Tornadoes

Titles in the Natural Disasters series include:

Natural **Disasters**

Tornadoes

by Andrew A. Kling

LUCENT BOOKS
SAN DIEGO, CALIFORNIA

THOMSON

™
GALE

Detroit • New York • San Diego • San Francisco
Boston • New Haven, Conn. • Waterville, Maine
London • Munich

Library of Congress Cataloging-in-Publication Data

Kling, Andrew A.
    Tornadoes / by Andrew A. Kling.
        p. cm. — (Natural disasters)
    Includes bibliographical references and index.
    Summary: Discusses the natural phenomenon of torna-
does including their development, the destruction they
cause, our ability to predict them, scientific studies, and efforts to educate and warn the public.
    ISBN 1-56006-977-5 (hardback : alk. paper)
        1. Tornadoes—Juvenile literature. [1. Tornadoes.] I.
Title. II. Natural disasters (Lucent Books)
        QC955.2 .K34 2002
        551.55'3—dc21

2001006946

Copyright © 2002 by Lucent Books,
an imprint of The Gale Group
10911 Technology Place, San Diego, CA 92127

Printed in the U.S.A.

Contents

Foreword

Fear and fascination are the two most common human responses to nature's most devastating events. People fear the awesome force of an earthquake, a volcanic eruption, a hurricane, and other natural phenomena with good reason. An earthquake can reduce multistory buildings to rubble in a matter of seconds. A volcanic eruption can turn lush forests and glistening lakes into a gray, flat landscape of mud and ash. A hurricane can lift houses from their foundations and hurl trucks and steel beams through the air.

As one witness to Hurricane Andrew, which hit Florida in 1992, recounts: "After the storm, planks and pieces of plywood were found impaling the trunks of large palms. . . . Eighteen-foot-long steel and concrete tie beams with roofs still attached were carried more than 150 feet. Paint was peeled from walls and street signs were sucked out of the ground and hurled through houses. Flying diesel fuel drums were a hazard, as were signs, awnings, decks, trash barrels, and fence posts that filled the skies. Mobile homes not only blew apart during the storm but disintegrated into aluminum shrapnel that became embedded in surrounding structures."

Fear is an understandable response to an event such as this, but it is not the only emotion people experience when caught in the throes of a natural disaster or when news of one blares from radios or flashes across television screens. Most people are fascinated by natural forces that have the power to claim life, crush homes, tear trees from their roots, and devastate whole communities—all in an instant. Why do such terrible events as these fascinate people? Perhaps the answer lies in humanity's inability to control them, and in the knowledge that they will recur—in some cases without warning—despite the scientific community's best efforts to understand and predict them.

A great deal of scientific study has been devoted to understanding and predicting natural phenomena such as earthquakes, volcanic eruptions, and hurricanes. Geologists and seismologists monitor the earth's motion from thousands of locations around the world. Their sensitive instruments record even the slightest shifts in the large tectonic plates that make up the earth's crust. Tools such as these have greatly improved efforts to predict natural disasters. When Mt. Pinatubo in the Philippines awoke from its six-hundred-year slumber in 1991, for example, a team of scientists armed with seismometers, tiltmeters, and personal computers successfully predicted when the volcano would explode.

Clearly, the scientific community has made great strides in knowledge and in the ability to monitor and even predict some of nature's most catastrophic events. Prediction techniques have not yet been perfected, however, and control of these events eludes humanity entirely. From the moment a tropical disturbance forms over the ocean, for example, researchers can track its progress and follow every twist in its path to becoming a hurricane but they cannot predict with certainty where it will make landfall. As one researcher writes: "No one knows when or where [a catastrophic hurricane] will strike, but we do know that eventually it will blast ashore somewhere and cause massive destruction. . . . Since there is nothing anyone can do to alter that foreboding reality, the question is: Are we ready for the next great hurricane?"

The many gaps in knowledge, coupled with the inability to control these events and the certainty that they will recur, may help explain humanity's continuing fascination with natural disasters. The Natural Disasters series provides clear and careful explanations, vivid examples, and the latest information about how and why these events occur, what efforts are being made to predict them, and to prepare for them. Annotated bibliographies provide readers with ideas for further research. Fully documented primary and secondary source quotations enliven the text. Each book in this series provides students with a wealth of information as well as launching points for further study.

Introduction

Xenia, Ohio,
April 3, 1974

On April 3, 1974, a tornado, a half mile wide, slammed into Xenia, Ohio. Railroad cars of a freight train passing through town were thrown across streets. The tornado smashed homes and businesses. It also demolished Central High School, just an hour after most students had left for the day. A teacher and students rehearsing a play in the school's auditorium escaped just seconds before the tornado threw two school buses through the walls and onto the stage.

The devastation was unbelievable, but the loss of life could have been much worse. For on April 2, 1974, National Weather Service forecasters studying weather patterns across the United States had concluded that the next day would bring potentially dangerous weather to parts of the nation. A low-pressure system was forming east of the Rocky Mountains; computer forecasts predicted it would strengthen as it moved east, pushing dry air eastward across the Mississippi River and pulling warm, humid air up from the Gulf of Mexico. Combined with another computer prediction for 100-mile-an-hour winds in the upper atmosphere's jet stream, the meteorologists realized the conditions were ripe for severe thunderstorms—the kind that generate the most dangerous tornadoes.

They were correct in their predictions, but in 1974 the best the forecasters could do was to send out their warnings by Teletype or telephone and hope that radio and television stations would spread the word. Consequently, when the storms hit on April 3 and 4, many Americans were unaware that they were in danger.

A tornado slams into Xenia, Ohio, in 1974, causing millions of dollars in damage.

The danger spread as thunderstorms raced along a line from Alabama to Ohio. By the time they dissipated in the early hours of April 4, the thunderstorms and tornadoes of the "Super Outbreak" (as it became known) had caused more than $600 million in damages. Three hundred and fifteen people had been killed; more than six thousand were injured; and more than twenty-seven thousand families suffered some kind of loss.

When the National Weather Service sent a team of investigators to see what had happened, they discovered that so many people had survived because of education:

> The people . . . heard weather watches and warnings over radio and television; were notified by their neighbors, relatives or friends; saw the tornadoes approaching; or heard the ominous roar of the tornado. . . . But most important,

they knew what to do when the time came to take action. They all seemed to know that a basement, if they had one, was the best place to be. . . . They got out of gymnasiums and large open rooms, stayed away from windows, protected their heads from flying debris.[1]

The Super Outbreak led to improvements in forecasting, computer models, and communications of approaching storms. The National Weather Service expanded its efforts to educate and train citizens about severe weather. New generations of scientists applied new technologies to investigate tornadoes. Thanks to them, the citizens of Xenia, Ohio, today have advance warnings available from radio, cable and satellite television, the Internet, and instant faxes . . . because the next tornado may be only a day away.

The Coming Fury

Tornadoes are nature's most destructive storms. The sheer force of these whirlwinds is the subject of myth and legend among scientists and survivors, because tornadoes are like no other force on earth. Unlike an earthquake, which can spread damage over hundreds of miles, a tornado's fury is concentrated to a specific location. Unlike a hurricane, which generally only affects coastal areas, a tornado can occur anywhere. Unlike a wildfire, which can be contained or extinguished, a tornado can neither be contained nor extinguished given the current state of science. Unlike a flood, which is often a gradual process of rising waters and increasing damage, a tornado strikes quickly, inflicts its damage, and is gone.

Each year more and more stories from those in the path of a tornado are shared with friends, family, colleagues, and amateur and professional tornado enthusiasts. These stories will long outlast the duration of the storms themselves, but they can help to unlock some of the secrets of tornadoes.

Even though thousands of tornadoes are born around the world each year, only recently have scientists been able to study the storms' mechanics and behavior. Because tornadoes are born, strike, and die in a relatively short period of time, it is often difficult for scientists to be in the right place at the right time in order to study them up close. But that does not prevent men and women across the world from seeking out, chasing, and studying tornadoes, and attempting to reproduce them in laboratories and with computers. Their efforts have led to outstanding investigations, predictions, and aftermath studies. Thanks to their efforts, those who live in areas of the United States most prone to tornadoes now have a better chance of learning if a tornado may be on the way.

Tornado Timetables

The word "tornado" is a form of the Spanish verb *tornar*, or "to turn," and another Spanish word, *tronada*, or "thunderstorm." Understanding the word's origins helps explain a tornado's origins and its behavior. Since tornadoes and thunderstorms are closely linked, an examination of tornadoes can begin with thunderstorms.

Knowing when a tornado may be on the way begins with knowledge of the seasons. Tornadoes form when the atmosphere is warm enough to support the development of thunderstorms, which begins with the coming of spring. As the earth's rotation around the sun brings the Northern Hemisphere closer to the sun's warmth, the atmosphere

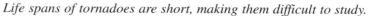

Life spans of tornadoes are short, making them difficult to study.

warms and becomes more likely to interact with areas that are still cooled with winter's chill. Therefore, the prime season for thunderstorms in the Northern Hemisphere begins in February or March and continues into October or November.

Further, thunderstorms are most common during the late afternoon and early evening. However, if the air remains warm enough at night, thunderstorms and tornadoes may form after dark.

Indeed, thunderstorms can exist in any season and at any time of day. For example, residents of the St. Louis, Missouri, area experienced severe thunderstorms that generated tornadoes in January 1989. The following day it snowed. But such January storms are the exception rather than the rule. Weather forecasters, scientists, and storm spotters know what time of year thunderstorms are most likely to form in their area. They know when to be on the alert for potential storm formation. And in order to determine if a tornado is on the way, weather observers look first to the clouds in the sky.

Weather Ingredients

Investigating tornadoes begins with investigating clouds, because clouds are the nurseries in which tornadoes are born. The vast majority of clouds will not generate tornadoes; tornadoes develop only under a certain set of conditions and only through the interaction of certain atmospheric conditions.

Three basic ingredients are needed for tornado formation: warm, moist air; cold, dry air; and warm, dry air. These are most often found in the United States in the area of the Great Plains, the large expanse of open and relatively flat land in the center of the country. Yet, according to Roger Edwards of the Storm Prediction Center of the National Oceanic and Atmospheric Administration (NOAA), "the classic answer [to how tornadoes form]—'warm moist Gulf [of Mexico] air meets cold Canadian air and dry air from the Rockies'—is a gross oversimplification."[2] In the same way a cook knows that too much of an ingredient will spoil the overall taste of a fine recipe, scientists know that only the right amount of each ingredient in the atmosphere will lead to a tornado. But, as Thomas P. Grazulis of the Tornado Project admits, scientists "do not know the recipe with which nature combines them."[3]

Scientists do know that when air masses with different temperatures come in contact with one another, masses of warm air will rise over banks of cold air, and moist air will sink below drier air. They also know that as sunlight heats the ground or water, warm, moist air rises into higher altitudes in the atmosphere, where the air pressure is lower. As the air mass moves into the low-pressure area, it expands and cools, a process that eventually turns the water vapor in the air into water droplets. A collection of water vapor droplets forms a cloud.

Clouds come in several different types, but the one that most concerns tornado investigators are cumulus clouds. A cumulus cloud ("cumulus" means heaped or stacked) usually has a base from 3,000 to 7,000 feet off the ground, and under the right conditions, may have a top that towers to a height of 30,000 to 50,000 feet. But, generally, above that height the cloud can no longer rise, as the water molecules turn to ice or snow in the cold stratosphere, and upper-level winds make it impossible for the warmer air to rise any higher. These winds create an inversion cap, which flattens the cloud top so that it looks like an anvil. The cumulus cloud has now been transformed into a thunderstorm cloud.

Inside this thunderstorm cloud, currents of air are continually in motion. The rising column of air (called an updraft) that has contributed to the cloud's formation eventually gets cut off in the upper atmosphere by upper-level winds, which turn the updraft into a downdraft. The downdraft helps wring the moisture out of the cloud, and most cumulus clouds will eventually rain themselves out of moisture before any severe weather develops. But because cumulus clouds usually occur in groups, rather than as individual clouds, often as a particular cloud dissipates, another is formed. In this way, the cycles of updrafts and downdrafts may continue for hours.

Closer to the ground, other forces are at work within the thunderstorm that may lead to tornado formation. Scientists

Cumulus clouds can tower up to a height of fifty thousand feet. Tornadoes form in this type of cloud.

are still studying exactly how a thunderstorm becomes a home to a tornado, but the latest evidence points to the behavior of a thin layer of air near the earth's surface as being a key to the genesis of tornadic winds.

The Winds Start to Spin

This thin layer of air near the ground surface is located in front of the advancing thunderstorms. It is highly vulnerable to disturbances caused by the phenomenon called wind shear, or changes in wind speed and direction at the top and bottom of the layer. As this thin layer of air moves toward the thunderstorm to replace air displaced by the storm's updraft, a sudden shift in the wind may shear, or cut off, the upper part of the layer. For example, the air a few thousand feet above the ground may be subject to fast-moving winds from the southwest, while the same layer of air just above the ground surface may be experiencing slower winds from the southeast. Under these conditions, parts of the layer are being pushed horizontally in different directions and at different speeds.

Erik Rasmussen and Paul Markowski of the National Severe Storms Laboratory explain the horizontal rotation in this way:

> Imagine what would happen if you put a paddlewheel in the atmosphere. It's easiest to think about this if the wind is all from the same direction. For example, if there are light west winds near the ground and strong west winds in the upper part of the atmosphere, the paddlewheel will rotate. We call this *horizontal* rotation because the axis of the paddlewheel is horizontal . . . aligned with the ground. This same idea works for any wind directions, and there is even horizontal rotation present because the wind changes direction as you go upward. . . . Now, what would happen if we take this air with horizontal rotation and turn it upwards into a thunderstorm updraft? We call this "tilting." The answer is that the rotation gets changed from horizontal . . . like an axle, to vertical . . . like a top. The rotation is further increased because the air rises faster and faster as you go up in the storm, and this has the same effect as a spinning skater bringing in their arms and spinning faster.[4]

In the atmosphere, wind shear has started to move the air in the same way that the paddle wheel is moving. The warm air, which has acquired a spinning motion parallel to the ground, is now in the form that scientists call a column. This column

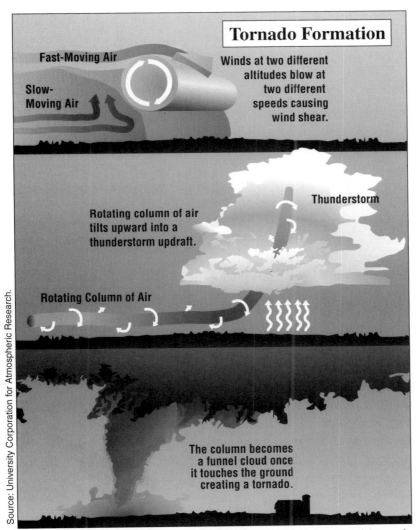

Source: University Corporation for Atmospheric Research.

Tornado Formation

Fast-Moving Air

Slow-Moving Air

Winds at two different altitudes blow at two different speeds causing wind shear.

Rotating column of air tilts upward into a thunderstorm updraft.

Thunderstorm

Rotating Column of Air

The column becomes a funnel cloud once it touches the ground creating a tornado.

is invisible to the naked eye and can only be detected by scientific instruments. But these rotating columns of air act much in the same way as rotating columns of water, such as those that occur in a sink or a bathtub drain, but they are harder to observe.

Air and water are both fluids. In the same way that a column of water from a draining sink changes shape as the amount of water in the sink changes, the rotating column of air near the face of a thunderstorm also changes. The air mass is constantly changing shape and usually moving in more than one direction at once. Therefore, while wind shear has been experienced (most notably when airplanes are caught in it), it is difficult to observe and measure. But its presence within a thunderstorm may be a forecast of changing conditions.

Changes in the Thunderstorm

A thunderstorm will grow in strength if the storm has a continuous source of energy. If warm, humid air stops flowing into the storm to replace air displaced by upper-level winds, the remaining moisture in the storm will fall as rain or hail and the thunderstorm will dissipate. But if warm, humid air continues to flow into the storm system, the thunderstorm lives on. If the storm's energy drain (in the form of downdrafts and precipitation) is equaled or exceeded by the thunderstorm's energy gain (in the form of continuing updrafts of warm, humid air), the thunderstorm will grow in size and strength.

As the storm continues to grow, the inversion cap may be broken. Rising air currents hurtle skyward, bulging the horizontally rotating column of air upward, and sometimes the column of air that was generated by the wind shear is broken into two columns, which then rotate side by side. The rotation of the air of these columns now becomes vertical within the updraft. If you were able to look down from the top of these columns, you would see that one column is rotating clockwise and the other is rotating counterclockwise. Scientists call this rotation vorticity, and the center of the rotation is called the vortex. The column rotating clockwise creates a system of high air pressure; the other, rotating counterclockwise, creates a system of low pressure called a mesocyclone. When observed by radar devices, a thunderstorm's mesocyclone shows up as a well-defined area of rotation, and most weather observers consider this to be a prelude to a tornado.

Not every thunderstorm will generate a tornado. Many bring thunder, lightning, and heavy rain, and sometimes more severe weather such as hail and strong winds. Scientists are

Waterspouts: A Different Kind of Windstorm

Waterspouts are windstorms that occur over water and that look and behave remarkably similar to tornadoes. They tend to live longer than tornadoes, but—according to Roger Edwards of the NOAA's Storm Prediction Center in "The Online Tornado FAQ: Frequently Asked Questions About Tornadoes" (www.spc.noaa.gov/faq/tornado)—waterspouts "don't officially count in tornado records unless they hit land. They are smaller and weaker than the most intense Great Plains tornadoes, but can still be quite dangerous. Water-spouts can overturn small boats, damage ships, do significant damage when hitting land, and kill people." Waterspouts can occur worldwide, just like land-based tornadoes, and can happen over seas, bays, and lakes.

This windstorm is considered a waterspout since it is occurring over water.

Joseph Golden, a senior meteorologist at NOAA, began his study of waterspouts in the 1960s. Today he and other meteorologists use helicopters to study these phenomena. But occasionally he discovers that nonscientists are also drawn to these sights. A NOAA news release, available on the Boating Channel Website, documents one such incident. In August 2000, when Golden and other scientists were photographing a waterspout, they were shocked to discover they were not alone in the area. "We watched in horrified amazement as a large outboard [boat] got to the spray vortex just as it was weakening," he said later. "It's only pure luck there haven't been more accidents. It's only a matter of time."

still studying how and why tornadoes develop in some thunderstorms and not in others. However, by continuing to observe thunderstorms and tornadoes, and by developing computer-based and mathematics-based models, they have learned a great deal about what tornadoes do and what they do not do.

Tornado Myths, Legends, and Truths

Some of what we read and what we hear about tornadoes comes from nonscientific sources. Sometimes the news about a tornado comes from someone who was not there, is not familiar with tornadoes, and has never studied them. In other cases, the source is exaggerating the effects of these storms just for fun. Consider this account of what tornadoes can do, according to a Canadian newspaperman: "[Tornadoes can] turn a well inside out, a cellar upside down, blow the staves out of a barrel leaving only the hole, change the day of the week, blow the cracks out of a fence, and knock the wind out of a politician."[5] Other accounts of tornadoes record an iron jug being blown inside out and a rooster being flung into a jug with only its head sticking out. An iron water hydrant was "supposedly full of splinters," and five horses were blown by a tornado a quarter of a mile from their barn, where they were eventually found "still hitched to the same rail,"[6] unhurt.

Such colorful accounts pique our interest about tornadoes, but they are not helpful in helping us to learn about what actually happens during a tornado. With the great amount of stories that exist surrounding tornadoes, anyone interested in studying them needs to be able to separate fact from fiction. This is often difficult, since sometimes what seems like a truly fantastic and impossible story may actually have a bit of truth in it.

For example, an often-repeated tale concerns chickens found among the debris after a tornado has passed through a farmyard. Depending on the tornado's behavior, the chicken coops may or may not have been damaged or destroyed. But invariably, the chickens in the story are found without their feathers, leading a reporter or an observer to suggest that the

The effects of tornadoes are sometimes hard to believe. This vehicle was picked up, flung into a tree, and stripped to its frame by the force of a tornado.

chickens' feathers had exploded from the effects of the tornado's low-pressure system. What is more likely is that the feathers came off due to an evolutionary trait among chickens. When a chicken is undergoing stress while being pursued by an enemy, such as a fox, some feathers will come loose so that the fox may end up with a mouthful of feathers instead of a mouthful of chicken. Scientists hypothesize that chickens caught up in the path of a tornado experience such a tremendous amount of stress that the animal loses *all* its feathers, which then are blown away in the tornado's winds.

Tornadoes in the Movies

In other cases, separating fantasy from fact can be more confusing because of the wide distribution of filmed depictions of

The Magic of *Twister*

In response to the depictions of tornadoes and storm chasers in *Twister*, Warner Brothers Studios established a website on the Internet that deals with many of the issues raised in the film, along with interviews of the cast and crew (movies.warnerbros. com/twister/cmp/swirl.html).

Among the crew responsible for the creation of the film were two second-crew units, whose jobs were to film the special cloud formations that were used as backdrops to the story. According to Ian Bryce, the film's producer, they raced across the Oklahoma and Iowa countryside to "chase a storm for a week and come back with some great footage."

Yet some of the most intense action scenes of the actors encountering storms had to be created through special effects. In one scene the crew imitated the windswept hail of a tornado using two ice chippers and a jet engine. The special effects supervisor explained, "We had to design a completely new machine that would crush ice small enough not to hurt the actors," and the jet engine was used to blast the ice chips at the actors in their vehicle during the scene.

Actors Bill Paxton and Helen Hunt in a scene from the film Twister.

fictional events. Motion pictures excel in portraying make-believe incidents in ways that make them seem real. Millions of people around the world have seen a tornado featured in the classic 1939 film *The Wizard of Oz*. More recently the film *Twister* created a story about scientists who study tornado formation, using a device called "DOROTHY," after the young girl supposedly swept away by a tornado in the earlier film. Both of these films present aspects about tornadoes that are factually possible and some that are truly mythical—in other words, that are the result of someone's imagination.

Because *The Wizard of Oz* was created before the days of network television, most Americans had never experienced a tornado and none had seen one on a TV newscast. Thus while the filmmakers had the challenge of making their tornado look realistic, they also knew that few members of the public would have enough familiarity with how tornadoes look to dispute the filmmakers' vision. Consequently they felt free to add a few touches to enhance the story. As often happens when fact and fantasy are mixed, sometimes the fantasy becomes seen as fact.

For example, it is true that, as shown in the film, many residents of Kansas take shelter from tornadoes in storm cellars dug into the earth that cannot be blown away by a tornado. However, the scene in which cows and old ladies riding bicycles become airborne and continue to stay upright even in the midst of the storm is pure fantasy. And, of course, houses are not lifted off their foundations in one piece. In the real world, a house caught by a tornado may lose its roof or be completely destroyed, with pieces landing dozens or hundreds of feet away. But given the public's lack of familiarity with the actual behavior of tornadoes and their interaction with man-made structures, the flying house effect was not only visually awesome but also believable to many people.

By the time *Twister* was released in 1996, tornadoes were a larger part of most filmgoers' experiences. Tornadoes are shown on television and the Internet with great frequency, and stories about them circulate widely in newspapers, magazines, and on radio broadcasts. However, the contributions of scientists studying tornadoes in the field, sometimes within the paths of the storms, are less well-known. Therefore, the creators of *Twister* had some of the same challenges as their *Oz* colleagues over fifty years earlier: Make the tornadoes real enough so that they are believable, but also make them powerful and awe-inspiring. With the help of computer-aided special effects, fact and fantasy are mixed, and sometimes the fantasy is presented as fact.

It is a fact that tornadoes have overturned vehicles and farm equipment. But no recorded tornado has ever lifted a fully loaded tanker tractor-trailer and thrown it to the ground, causing it to explode in a ball of flame. *Twister*'s filmmakers accurately portrayed the propensity of tornadoes to strike with little or no warning. However, the film tended to identify each and every occurrence of rotational winds as tornadoes. By definition, a tornado is "a rapidly rotating column of air in contact with the earth's surface."[7] "In contact with the earth's surface" is an important distinction, which can be used to dispel the myth that a tornado may skip over a house, field, or neighborhood and then strike another nearby. "Skipping tornadoes" simply do not exist. "A tornado *must* be in contact with the ground," according to Roger Edwards of NOAA's Storm Prediction Center. When the rotating cloud is not in contact with the ground, "it is literally no longer a tornado." Even if the same column of air makes ground contact later, "it is a separate tornado."[8]

Windstorms Around the World

Other sources of confusion about tornadoes occur when they are compared to other windstorms, such as hurricanes and typhoons. Tornadoes are similar to hurricanes and typhoons in that all are cyclonic storms, that is, storms that involve winds that rotate about a center. But unlike hurricanes and typhoons, tornadoes have a relatively short life cycle. Tropical storms—cyclonic storms that occur over the water, such as hurricanes and typhoons—can last for weeks at a time. As long as they have access to a source of energy in the form of warm air up-lifting from warm open water, they will continue to maintain or even increase their strength.

But unlike waterborne storms, tornadoes are short-lived and spend most of their life over land. Because, in general, just three ingredients need to be present for tornadoes to form (warm, moist air; cold, dry air; and warm, dry air), and because the earth's atmosphere is constantly in motion, it is inevitable that from time to time these ingredients will combine in various places across the world.

The clash of these three ingredients occurs with great frequency within the continental United States, and tornadoes occur in the greatest numbers there, especially in the states of Texas, Oklahoma, Kansas, and Nebraska. Tornadoes have been recorded in all fifty states; Florida has the highest number of

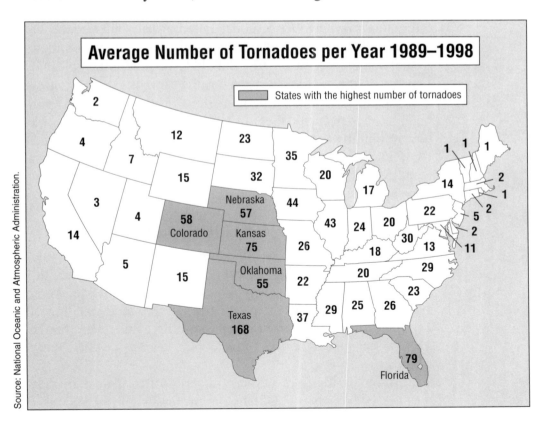

Average Number of Tornadoes per Year 1989–1998

States with the highest number of tornadoes

Source: National Oceanic and Atmospheric Administration.

tornadoes per square mile per year, and Oklahoma has the second highest percentage. (Texas ranks tenth, but Texas has much more land area than Florida.) Further, the highest number of destructive tornadoes per year occurs in Oklahoma. This has led to a belief that tornadoes occur only in North America. The large number of tornadoes is in large part due to the nation's geography, but it is also due in part to the system of weather forecasting that might record tornadoes that might be missed elsewhere.

But tornadoes do occur elsewhere around the world. Tornadoes have also been recorded in Europe. According to one researcher, the earliest recorded tornado occurred in London, England, in 1091: "Two men were killed when the storm raised the roof at a church. About six hundred houses were damaged."[9] Bangladesh seems to have the most dangerous and deadly tornadoes outside of the United States. Three tornadoes on October 5, 2001, killed at least ten people, injured at least a thousand, and destroyed as many as ten thousand homes. According to a Bangladeshi government official, many of the victims were returning from services in local mosques. Additionally, perhaps the world's most deadly single tornado occurred there in 1989. "As many as 1,300 people were initially reported killed and 12,000 injured as a tornado cut a long track, up to a mile wide. . . . The towns of Salturia and Manikganj were leveled, and about 80,000 people were made homeless."[10]

The Challenge for Tornado Scientists

Clearly, tornadoes are one of nature's most destructive forces. Each storm that brings widespread destruction becomes the subject of intense scrutiny by researchers worldwide. Their dedication has led to great advances in the understanding of tornado formation, development, and life cycle, even though all of the pieces of the tornado puzzle are not yet clearly known.

Following the devastation of a series of tornadoes in May 1999, University of Oklahoma professor of meteorology

Howard Bluestein remarked on the awesome nature of these storms, "We were seeing something we are not sure we understand . . . but I hope we will learn from it."[11]

Indeed, the ever-changing conditions within each thunderstorm and tornado system continue to challenge tornado scientists and enthusiasts. Thus, they continue to develop computer simulations, study data from previous tornadoes, and, above all, they continue to watch the skies for the signs of the coming fury.

Tornadogenesis: The Tornado Forms

Scientists and observers who study tornadoes have made great advancements in the last fifty years. They know that certain conditions need to be present for a tornado to form, although sometimes tornadoes will form when no development is expected. Because scientists and amateurs alike continue to be awed and fascinated by severe weather, they have forged a partnership that benefits both the scientific and the general populations. They combine proven techniques with new technologies to advance the study of tornadogenesis, or the formation of tornadoes.

The observations of both professionals and amateurs are instrumental in the study of tornadogenesis. Because tornadoes occur across the United States, and often in rural areas, sometimes the only record of a tornado event comes from firsthand observation by nonscientists. The record may be a conversation, recollection, photograph, or home movie on videotape. The key to using this information in studying tornadogenesis lies in the interpretation of the evidence. In each case the story of the storm begins with what the observer saw in the sky.

Keep Your Eyes on the Skies

The oldest way to study the weather is to watch the skies. For centuries individuals have gazed skyward and tried to understand the mechanics of the atmosphere. Today weather watchers still use the ancient technique of observing with nothing more than a pair of eyes. Science has furthered our under-standing of what we see in the skies, and scientists now have a wide range of tools to aid our observations. But eyewitness accounts of the patterns of thunderstorms and tornadoes are still an important part of the study of tornadogenesis.

A person who watches the sky for approaching storms or changing weather conditions is called a storm spotter. Most storm spotters are amateur weather observers, who watch the

A storm spotter watches a storm develop in the distance. Observations made by storm spotters help scientists study tornadoes.

skies on a volunteer basis and report to local weather stations. They report to various private organizations, such as television stations, or public organizations, such as sheriffs' offices. Storm spotters who watch the skies for approaching thunderstorms that may lead to tornadoes know when and where to look, based on current weather reports, forecasts, and their own experience and training.

The spotters have been trained to interpret the patterns they see in the skies. Many have years of experience in observing thunderstorm formations. They know to concentrate their efforts on watching the skies in the direction of approaching weather systems and during the months when severe thunderstorms and tornadoes are most common in their area. With no specialized equipment or high-tech devices, they provide important input to weather professionals. They know that two important conditions can be reported by their direct observations: cloud formation and wind behavior.

Cloud Formation

Since cumulus clouds, which are the precursors of thunderstorms, lie at the heart of tornado formation, storm spotters watch thunderstorm clouds carefully. Early warning about several important formations can greatly assist the meteorologists who must analyze potentially severe weather systems.

The most severe weather comes from thunderstorm clouds with an overshooting top above the anvil head of the cloud. An overshooting top signifies that the updraft air currents have been able to push through the anvil cloud top. The National Weather Service (NWS) warns that spotters "should pay particular attention to a storm with an overshooting top since the area beneath the top is a preferred area for severe weather formation."[12] A large overshooting top that persists for more than ten minutes and an anvil with sharp, well-defined edges are usually signs of potentially severe weather.

Two more important features of a potentially severe thunderstorm system are the rain-free base and the wall cloud. A rain-free base as seen by a ground observer is "a dark, hori-

A wall cloud with a rain-free base indicates a severe thunderstorm and the possibility of a tornado.

zontal cloud base with no *visible* precipitation beneath it. It typically marks the location of the thunderstorm updraft."[13] The rain-free base may not actually be rain free, however; it may contain hail or large raindrops that are not visible to a storm spotter. A wall cloud is a local and often abrupt cloud lowering from a rain-free base. A National Oceanic and Atmospheric Administration (NOAA) publication cautions:

> Tornadoes may develop from wall clouds attached to the rain-free base, or from the rain-free base itself—especially when the rain-free base is on the south or southwest side of the main precipitation area. Wall clouds can range from a fraction of a mile up to nearly five miles in diameter, and normally are found on the south or southwest (inflow) side of the thunderstorm.[14]

When seen from a distance of several miles, many wall clouds display rapid upward-moving air as well as tornadic rotation.

Wind Behavior

Along with observations of cloud formations, weather observers remain on the alert for changes in wind behavior. Generally wind is more felt than seen, but careful observation of the surrounding environment can lead to visual clues about changes in wind behavior. Objects such as trees, bushes, and crops in the field, and areas such as dust-covered, freshly plowed fields, are excellent indicators of wind behavior. Although most changes in wind direction and speed occur above ground level, there are certain phenomena that spotters need to be able to recognize. The most important of these are downbursts.

Downbursts are strong downdrafts from a thunderstorm resulting in an outrush of damaging winds on or near ground level. They can suddenly flatten bushes, topple trees, or create dense clouds of rapidly moving dust. Downbursts alone are *not* an indication of tornado activity. But the speed of the wind, and the damage it may produce, may cause observers to confuse downbursts with tornadoes. The most important distinction between a downburst and a tornado lies in rotation: a downburst's winds travel in a straight line without rotation. Downbursts are much more common than tornadoes, and experienced spotters can distinguish between the two.

Storm Spotters and Their Contributions to Science

In addition to their community-based efforts across the country, storm spotters have added to scientists' understanding of severe storm formation and tornado behavior. In the last sixty years, storm spotters have made tremendous contributions to science with their observations, and scientists continue to enlist their expertise in studying developing storms.

The first organized network of storm spotters was recruited during World War II. Meteorologist Charles Doswell notes that at first the spotters' "primary concern was for lightning near ordnance [ammunition] plants, but the program grew substantially during the war and the mission of the spotters was expanded to include other hazardous weather, including tornadoes. . . . [B]y June, 1945, there were more than 200 observer networks in place around the country."[15] The state of Texas responded to several disastrous tornadoes in the 1950s by establishing the Texas Radar Tornado Warning network, which also incorporated volunteer storm spotters. By the mid-1950s, such networks of spotters were becoming common-place and were assisting forecasters and scientists in the field of tornadogenesis.

For example, a network of storm spotters was instrumental in the development of the supercell theory of thunderstorm behavior. In 1959 British scientist Frank Ludlam and his student Keith Browning organized over two thousand volunteers to serve as storm spotters and assist them in their tornado

A storm spotter unloads camera equipment as a storm develops in the distance. Networks of storm spotters are in place today to help gather tornado data for scientists and weather forecasters.

studies. The network paid off on July 9, 1959, as seven severe thunderstorms crossed southern England, with one of them passing directly over Ludlam and Browning's observatory and radar installation. The scientists coordinated their radar data with the observations of the storm spotters, who had recorded the events and life cycles of the storms with great precision. The spotters' minute-by-minute observations al-

Supercells

The study of severe weather is like the study of any other subject. In order to communicate advancements in understanding, students need to develop a common language and understand common concepts. In the study of tornadogenesis, an important addition is the concept of the supercell. Scientists now recognize that supercells are key ingredients in thunderstorms that lead to formations of tornadoes.

The supercell is a relatively recent concept, when compared with how long humankind has been experiencing thunderstorms and tornadoes. In England in 1959, scientists were amazed when data indicated that a single thunderstorm system had stayed in an almost unchanged steady-state condition for over an hour. According to Thomas P. Grazulis in *The Tornado: Nature's Ultimate Windstorm*, "It was unheard of for something as chaotic and changeable as a thunderstorm to do this." He defines a supercell as a "constantly evolving heat engine that spawns and keeps alive the devastating tornadoes that appear at the top of the killer tornado lists."

Today supercells are recognized as the rule rather than the exception when it comes to severe thunderstorms. Single-cell thunderstorms—storms that grow, mature, and decay—are relatively rare. The most common type of thunderstorms are multicell thunderstorms, which are defined by Jack Williams in *The Weather Book* as "clusters of single-cell storms . . . [in which air] flowing outward from one storm can supply the upward push of warm, humid air needed to trigger other cells." But supercell storms are the ones that generate the most severe weather and most tornadoes.

A storm spotter watches the sky.

lowed Ludlam and Browning to develop a timeline for the storm's life cycle. Their supercell theory, which attributes the formation of most severe thunderstorms and tornadoes to a persistently rotating updraft, helps explain some of the unanswered questions about tornadic thunderstorms. And the assistance of the volunteer storm spotters may well have been essential to the development of this theory.

Today's storm spotters who work with the NWS are part of the SKYWARN network. Following a series of tornadoes known as the Palm Sunday Outbreak on April 11, 1965, several federal agencies coordinated the development of a nationwide network to broadcast disaster-related information. Part of this system was a plan called SKYWARN, which was

Doppler Radar

The use of radar systems in meteorology has become commonplace in the last thirty years. Basically, radar works like this: microwave radio signals emitted from a radar transmitter reflect off objects such as storm clouds and return to the radar unit. From the time it takes the signal to return to the radar unit, the operator can tell how far the object is from the radar unit.

As early as 1953, radar was providing meteorologists with insights into the formation and behavior of tornadoes, but the development of Doppler radar in the 1970s was a giant leap forward in the field. Doppler provides forecasters and scientists with an unprecedented look into the behavior and structure of storm systems and has been widely used in the observation of tornadoes.

In an article in *Scientific American* in August 1995, Robert Davies-Jones of the National Severe Storms Laboratory (NSSL) in Norman, Oklahoma, described how Doppler units work:

> Doppler weather radars measure wind speeds from afar by emitting pulses of microwave radiation and catching their reflections off a group of raindrops or ice particles. If the drops are moving toward the radar, the reflected pulse has a shorter wavelength that betrays this component of the drops' velocity. . . . The radar [cannot] "see" or resolve the tornado directly but [the Doppler system] showed high winds changing direction abruptly across the twister and its precursor in the clouds. This vortex signature typically forms at around 9,000 feet 10 to 20 minutes before touchdown.

Today the National Weather Service has a nationwide network of Doppler radar systems to provide severe storm information to even remote locations of the United States. In addition, many television stations have their own Doppler units for their broadcast area. Scientists now use Doppler units from airplanes and trucks to develop three-dimensional views of thunderstorms, mesocyclones, and tornadoes, and they have continued to further our knowledge of severe weather.

specifically designed for dealing with tornadoes. The NWS has been instrumental in SKYWARN's evolution; according to Doswell, "Over time, the NWS has accepted the responsibility for training severe weather spotters who volunteer to serve their communities by watching imminent severe weather events . . . most notably tornadoes."[16]

Today spotters continue to volunteer their time to alert communities and residents across the country about severe weather and tornado formation. Both urban and rural areas benefit from their expertise. In March 1997 storm spotters reported tornadoes in suburban Memphis, Tennessee. According to the NWS office, "A spotter report[ed] a tornado 14 miles southwest of Walnut Ridge. This prompted the tornado warning for Lawrence [County] issued at 3:59 P.M. The tornado touched down along highway 230 and moved east-northeast for about one and a half miles."[17] On the afternoon

The National Weather Service first experimented with Doppler radar using this unit. Today the Weather Service maintains a nationwide system.

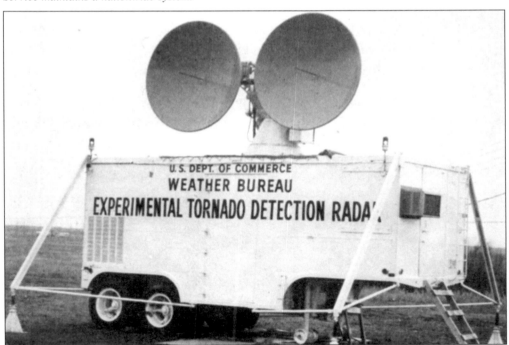

of July 19, 2001, a spotter in rural north-central South Dakota alerted the NWS to a potentially dangerous situation. According to Tim Kearns, an NWS manager, "A spotter said [the storm] produced a wall cloud and funnel cloud,"[18] although there was no verification that a tornado touched down. It is quite possible that the spotter in question was still on alert for severe weather since a tornado had caused damage in neighboring Tolstoy, South Dakota, the day before.

Trained storm spotters and other observers at ground level work in conjunction with meteorological professionals who interpret the information from the field spotters and from their own instruments to determine any weather threats. Many of these are electronic marvels, while others are less-sophisticated devices. Technologies from kites to computers have helped to further the study of tornadogenesis.

What Technology Can Tell Us About Tornadogenesis

Computers are increasingly a part of daily life, and weather scientists have taken advantage of each advance in computing speed, memory capacity, and graphic abilities. The first attempts to use computers to develop models of tornadogenesis came in the 1960s, and since then scientists have made great strides in trying to understand how thunderstorms and tornadoes form. They hope to eventually be able to explain through mathematical models and equations what takes place in the atmosphere.

Howard Bluestein of the University of Oklahoma notes that by the late 1970s, computers were able to simulate storm conditions given several different variables:

> While [meteorologists] Peter Ray, Joe Klemp, Bob Wilhelmson, and collaborators were attempting to simulate real storms in the late 1970s and early 1980s, meteorologists Morris Weisman and Joe Klemp began to explore the range of behavior that virtual storms might exhibit if idealized wind, temperature, and moisture fields were var-

ied systematically. . . . [They] ran three-dimensional models on a supercomputer with fascinating results, showing a striking relationship between storm type and vertical wind shear, on the one hand, and the amount of buoyancy in a storm's updraft, on the other. . . . Using the Weisman-Klemp scheme, one could look at real data [from field observations] and attempt to forecast the type of storm that would occur.[19]

Since then, other researchers have been able to simulate tornado vortices in simulated thunderstorms, as well as several fine-scale features of tornado behavior. Given the advancements in computer modeling since that time, Bluestein forecasts, "with more advanced computers, the numerical simulation of supercell storms, nonsupercell storms, and the tornadoes each of these spawns will soon be possible."[20]

However, computer models can only be based on what researchers have experienced in the real world. The information gathered from weather observers and meteorologists continues to provide the mathematical researchers with data that assist their modeling. Yet there are technologies predating computers that still assist severe weather and tornado researchers.

Kites, Rawinsondes, and Satellites

In the early part of the 1900s a man named Vincent Jakl combined an ages-old device with then current recording technology and succeeded in making a very important contribution to the knowledge of tornado behavior. For several years he had been flying kites with weather instruments at heights of up to two miles above Drexel, Nebraska. On the morning of March 20, 1920, he noticed an unusual condition during one of these flights. On the ground he experienced a warm wind from the south, but where his kite was, two miles high, colder air was blowing from the west. That afternoon nineteen killer tornadoes struck to the east of Drexel. Jakl succeeded in combining personal observation and technical data to conclude that

Weather balloons called rawinsondes are launched from weather stations in the United States twice a day to measure temperature and humidity in the upper atmosphere.

his observations and the storms were related. From that time forward, tornado outbreaks have been linked to airflows in the upper atmosphere.

Today professionals no longer use kites to measure conditions in the upper atmosphere. Instead, they launch balloons called rawinsondes that measure temperature and humidity. These balloons are called rawinsondes because their function includes *ra*dar, *win*d, and radio*sondes* (miniature transmitters). The rawinsondes record the information during their rise in the atmosphere and then radio the data back automatically to the ground. By tracking the rawinsondes' movements, scientists can also gauge wind speed and direction. Across the United States, these balloons are launched from weather stations twice a day, at 7 A.M. and 7 P.M. The information they return helps meteorologists construct a picture of the behavior of the upper atmosphere.

The information from rawinsondes launched nationwide helps the NWS put together a picture of conditions from coast to coast, and the patterns it suggests help form the forecasts broadcast on television and radio. For example, data from balloons launched from Colorado recording cool, dry air will help forecast conditions on the Great Plains for the coming days. In this way, forecasters can see the movement of air masses that may collide to form severe weather such as tornadoes.

For a larger-scale view of the atmosphere's behavior, scientists turn to satellites orbiting high above the earth. Geostationary satellites (those that orbit the earth at the same

Project VORTEX

In the spring of 1994 and 1995, scientists from the U.S. government and from universities across North America gathered to participate in Project VORTEX (short for "*V*erification of the *O*rigins of *R*otation in *T*ornadoes *Ex*periment"). The project mobilized unparalleled resources in personnel, vehicles on the ground and in the air, and the latest scientific equipment. Spearheaded by Erik Rasmussen of the National Severe Storms Laboratory at the National Oceanic and Atmospheric Administration (NOAA), the project tested and challenged current theories about tornadogenesis.

According to the NOAA's summary of the project (as reported on *USA Today*'s website at www.usatoday.com/weather/wvor2.htm), the project promises to offer insights into tornadogenesis for years to come.

VORTEX scientists collected data documenting the entire life cycle of a tornado. They expect this information will lead to important new insights into how tornadoes form, develop into full-fledged tornadoes, then dissipate. . . . One tornado intercepted by VORTEX, the Dimmitt, Texas, tornado of June 2, 1995, is now the most thoroughly observed tornado in history. VORTEX director Erik Rasmussen said, "VORTEX has been a huge success. But as a formal thing, VORTEX is no more. The data collection phase of the experiment is complete. The real work of analyzing and interpreting the data essentially is just beginning." VORTEX scientists speculate it will take years to make sense of all the data. But Rasmussen is confident the answer to tornado formation is in the data somewhere. . . . "We're probably [close to] having a real nice conceptual model of tornadogenesis. I think we'll eventually be rewriting some books on tornadoes," Rasmussen said.

As one theory of tornado formation gives way to another, scientists feel they are getting closer to understanding these fascinating storms. More than five years after the project concluded, scientists are still poring over the figures, the radar signatures, and the photographs. Perhaps the key to understanding tornadogenesis lies within.

speed as the planet's rotation, so that the satellites appear to be above the same location at all times) show the movement of cloud formations. The series of geostationary operational environmental satellites (GOES) sends back high-resolution photographs from twenty thousand miles above the earth. These photographs are a feature of many television weather broadcasts. Linking these photographs together, the forecasters can present a movie of clouds forming and dissipating and the movement of the jet stream as it moves from east to west and north to south across the country.

Data from the advanced technology of rawinsondes and satellites play important roles in the development of forecasts across the nation. Yet the key to all the tools at the disposal of scientists remains the forecasters' ability to make sense of all the numbers, photographs, and lines on a map, and to develop an accurate picture of the days to come.

The Art and Science of Prediction

The data from all the sources of information available to scientists can only give a broad picture of the nation's weather. But they can suggest areas that may experience severe weather based on the collision of air masses. For example, the National Weather Service correctly forecast a major outbreak of tornadoes in Oklahoma and Kansas on Friday, April 26, 1991. The forecast was based partly on patterns meteorologists saw in the data from sources like satellites and rawinsondes, and partly on the experience of the NWS professionals. The NWS recognized several days in advance that airflow, temperature, and humidity patterns were likely to create a dangerous situation over the Great Plains; thus as the patterns became clearer, the agency was able to issue alerts across the nation.

Although weather forecasting remains an inexact science, and weather predictions for as little as twenty-four hours in advance can be inaccurate, the NWS's analysis of the atmospheric patterns on Sunday, April 21, 1991, had suggested severe weather for the end of the coming week.

Despite advances in technology, the ability to predict tornadoes is not an exact science. Meteorologists have learned how to recognize weather patterns that might develop into tornadoes and issue broad warnings to the public.

As soon as the NWS alerted the regional NWS stations about the broader patterns of the atmosphere's behavior that week, local forecasters focused their attention on the potential danger areas.

By the early morning of Thursday, April 25, forecasters were concerned that tornadoes would develop across a wide area from Texas to Iowa within thirty-six hours. The long-term predictions based on patterns from data a week earlier were beginning to look more and more accurate. The NWS's

National Severe Storms Forecast Center (NSSFC) in Norman, Oklahoma, issued a two-day outlook that included an advisory warning that "tornado activity was likely ahead of a cold front that was forecast to move eastward across the central and southern plains on Friday afternoon and evening."[21]

Later that day the two-day outlook was updated, and the NSSFC said the potential existed for "a significant outbreak of tornadoes in the central United States"[22] the next day. Experienced local meteorologists, forecasters, and weather spotters understood that the NSSFC rarely used terms as potentially alarming as "significant outbreak" and began to focus their attention on every advisory and weather map that the NWS issued that day. By 7 P.M. on Thursday, it was apparent that an area from central Oklahoma to southeastern Nebraska was going to be in the bull's-eye.

Just seven hours later, at 2 A.M. on Friday, the NSSFC issued a one-day outlook. In the most severe language they had available, they warned of a "high risk" of "damaging tornadoes."[23] As predicted, tornadoes started forming a few hours later. The first ones, in Oklahoma, were relatively weak, and the thunderstorms from which they formed dissipated by noon. But large-scale conditions continued to worsen, and the first tornado watch was issued at 12:10 P.M. A tornado watch means that conditions are favorable for tornado development and usually covers a relatively small area of a state or region for a short period of time. But this watch covered almost all of central Kansas and was in effect for the next eight hours. It also warned of the danger of very damaging tornadoes.

The prediction was correct. Over the next twelve hours—into the early morning hours of April 27—tornadoes streaked across Oklahoma and Kansas. More than fifty tornadoes touched down, killing a total of twenty-one people.

The good news in an outbreak like this is that the damage and death tolls could have been much worse: a tornado in the same general area in 1955 killed over eighty people. The scientists in 1991 took advantage of the advances in technology to correctly interpret the atmospheric patterns. They used a combination of technological information and observational experience to understand the potential for tornadogenesis, to help alert residents in time to take the necessary precautions to deal with the severe weather.

Meeting the Challenge

Meteorologists had several challenges during the week of April 21–27, 1991. The first was to understand the patterns they were seeing in the atmosphere. The second was to be able to react in a timely fashion to the developing situation. The final challenge was to keep local officials and organizations informed about the impending severe weather. They succeeded in meeting each of these challenges.

Other scientists had challenges during that week as well. Men and women who study severe weather mobilized their forces to face the storms at close range. Armed with the latest technology and years of cumulative experience, these professionals and students race across the surrounding country from storm to storm in hopes that the next storm they are chasing will help them understand tornadogenesis just a little bit better, so that the next time a tornado threatens, area residents will have had plenty of time to prepare for potential danger.

The Tornado Strikes

When a tornado strikes, many people wish to be well out of the way. For dedicated teams of scientists across the country, however, the best way to observe and learn about tornadoes is to be as close to them as safely possible when they form and when they strike. To this end, these storm chasers venture out into the severe weather in order to gather data from various instruments and to record the storm with photographs and videotape.

On the Front Lines: Storm Chasers

Many storm chasers are professionals associated with colleges and universities or branches of the U.S. government, such as the National Severe Storms Laboratory (NSSL). Often these two segments of weather investigators work hand in hand to track storm formation. But because tornadoes are a rare event, there are many times when storm chasers venture out into severe weather conditions only to discover no tornadoes. Storm chaser Val Castor, who works for Oklahoma City television station KWTV, says that in over ten years of chasing, "in reality we only see a tornado every 10 to 12 times we go out. We just put a lot of hours in behind the wheel."[24] Researcher Howard Bluestein says, "Gathering information in the field and making split-second decisions are crucial to successful storm chasing. In effect, we act like an intelligence unit and make decisions based upon our atmospheric informants."[25]

In most cases storm chasers wish to get as close to severe thunderstorms and tornadoes as they can without endangering themselves or losing valuable equipment. But in some cases they get closer than they wish to be, either because the storm shifted unexpectedly or because there was no other choice. University of Oklahoma researcher Herb Stein describes a harrowing encounter with a storm in Oklahoma:

> We [drove] ahead, trying to escape the rain so we could witness the tornado, when suddenly the wind and debris picked up force. We heard a loud "thud" as something airborne hit the side of our truck. Branches and small articles were moving horizontally across the road, and the heavy rain—also moving horizontally—whited out our view of anything outside the truck. We stopped, and I could feel the truck being blown forward by the powerful

Storm chaser Gene Bertran checks his equipment in the cab of his truck (below). Bertran carries weather instruments and a video camera to capture tornado information. At right, Bertran checks wind speed with an anemometer.

winds. The rain was so intense it interfered with the radar signals. We measured the nearby winds, and found they were moving up to 100 miles an hour. As our 13-ton truck rocked in the winds, it was filled with a low-frequency noise as the wind rushed across our equipment. My mouth went completely dry as I contemplated my arrogance in wanting to keep driving into the teeth of the tornado. After what seemed like an eternity, the winds ebbed. We saw that a telephone pole had been bent over alongside our truck.[26]

Near Purcell, Oklahoma, in 1992, Castor encountered a rain-wrapped tornado that passed within a hundred yards of his vehicle. Tree limbs and other debris passed overhead at an estimated hundred miles an hour. He has seen lightning strike as close as twenty feet and hail as large as softballs, "smashing car windshields and bouncing 8 feet off the ground"[27] during other chases.

The time that storm chasers spend in actual contact with tornadoes is very small when compared with the amount of time they spend in pursuit of storms. But as the men and women on the front lines of tornado contact, they have contributed a great deal to science. Their data, along with firsthand reports from tornado survivors and computer models, have led scientists to a better understanding of what happens when a tornado strikes.

Inside the Whirlwind

When a tornado strikes, the rotating column of air that touches down on the ground may cause little noticeable damage or may lead a swath of destruction behind for all to see. There are untold numbers of accounts of survivors who have lived through tornadoes as they passed near or over their homes, farms, or vehicles, and many of them have certain details in common.

The most common detail these accounts have in common concerns the tornado's shape. The typical funnel cloud shape

From a distance, a tornado appears in the typical funnel cloud shape. Up close, witnesses report being able to see debris caught in the whirlwind.

of tornadoes seen at a distance becomes much more detailed when witnessed up close. Survivors tell of seeing debris of all shapes and sizes caught in the whirlwind. If the path of the tornado brought it across open country, the debris may consist of dust and dirt and objects ripped from the ground along its track, such as sections of fencing. But if the path has gone over homes or other structures, the debris will include pieces of wood, paper and plastic, shards of glass and metal, and roofing materials. The weight of the debris is directly related to the storm's power; the stronger the tornado, the heavier the items are that it can capture.

The sound of the tornado often becomes ingrained in survivors' memories. Some say they heard a sound like a freight train as the tornado approached. Other witnesses recount that the tornado made a whooshing sound, like a waterfall. Each of these sounds, according to the Storm Prediction Center's Roger Edwards, "depends on what [the tornado] is hitting, its size, its intensity, closeness and other factors. . . . Tornadoes which are tearing through densely populated areas may be producing all kinds of loud noises at once, which collectively may make a tremendous roar."[28] In such a scenario, as a powerful tornado moves through an urban or suburban area, survivors may be hearing the noises of downed electrical lines

One Family's Story—Kansas, 1932

On May 25, 1932, on a farm in northwestern Kansas, John Newport watched the skies over his wheat fields as the leading edge of an enormous thunderstorm passed overhead. There had been a good deal of lightning but only a brief shower of rain. As the worst seemed over, Newport returned to his chores. However, he soon heard a muffled roar in the distance that grew sharper and louder as he stood and listened. He realized that the low, indistinct form in the distance was a huge tornado. It was unlike any he had seen before, and it was headed straight for his farm and his family. He ran full speed to his house, yelling, "Cyclone!"

The rest of the story is recounted by the Tornado Project's director, Thomas Grazulis, and can be found on the Tornado Project's website, www.tornadoproject.com:

With the edge of the vortex still to the southwest, the corner of the roof suddenly gave way and the 30-year-old cottonwood trees that surrounded the house began to snap. . . . [T]he entire building vibrated as the unearthly roar grew steadily louder.

. . . The storm cave [the family's designated shelter], dug some distance from the house, was now out of reach behind a growing wall of flying debris. The root cellar was the only remaining refuge. The children went first, the mother grabbing each by the arm, and quickening their movement. . . . The father braced himself against the kitchen door. The last child was on the steps when and poles, uprooted trees and flying branches, displaced roofs, and crashing walls, all combining in a deafening cacophony.

Will Keller of Kansas survived a tornado that passed over his farm in 1928. Before entering his storm shelter, he took the time to look up into the funnel cloud as it passed directly overhead. He said he heard a "screaming, hissing sound coming directly from the end of the funnel," and when the mouth of the funnel went over, he saw

a circular opening in the center of the funnel, about 50 or 100 feet in diameter, extending straight upward for a

the parents finally moved toward the cellar, but the first of the intense whirling columns had reached the house.

In later interviews, none of the children mentioned whether there was, between the parents, a final glance at one another. If there were final words at the top of the stairs, they were not heard above the deafening roar.

Winds in excess of 200 mph created a pressure of 20 tons on the side of the small farm house and the building finally reached its limit of resistance. In an instant, a lifetime of work . . . walls, beams, plaster, furniture, tools, clothes, toys, books, and family treasures were all airborne. Some would fall only a few hundred feet away; smaller bits and pieces would be carried 120 miles. . . . The 12-inch-thick hand-hewn sills, on which the house had sat for forty years, would hit the ground a quarter-mile away and plunge eight feet into the prairie soil. An entire cottonwood tree was found two miles away.

After a few minutes the children emerged from the cellar, not into the kitchen, but out into a rain and hail storm. They located the lifeless body of their mother about 100 yards from the empty foundation. The father, barely alive, was found 200 yards further away. . . . His last words were instructions to get to the nearest neighbor for help, a half mile away. He fell into unconsciousness in the arms of his eldest daughter. The children, Mildred, Martha, Eleanor, Dean, and Paul, ages 3–15, ran through a barrage of five-inch-diameter hail. They arrived at the next farm battered, bloodied, with broken arms and ribs. John died a few hours later in a neighbor's living room. The children began new lives with their grandparents.

distance of at least one half mile. . . . [T]he walls of this opening were of rotating clouds and the hole was made brilliantly visible by constant flashes of lightning which zigzagged from side to side.[29]

His account has a number of remarkable details that scientists have confirmed only recently through radar technology, such as the hole in the center of the funnel. However, scientists and emergency officials heartily discourage anyone from trying to duplicate Keller's unique observations.

The sound and fury of a tornado, along with the storm's unpredictable speed and direction, combine to create memorable eyewitness accounts among survivors. Since each person will remember the same event differently based on his or her own experience, researchers sometimes have a difficult time piecing together the storm's true size and strength. For example, scientists can estimate how strong the winds were inside the tornado Will Keller saw, but the figure will never be more than an educated guess. Today's technology can help meteorologists compile better, more accurate statistics of tornadoes they observe at present, but sometimes technology is not enough to further their investigations.

Some Tornado Statistics

Even with all the technology available, it is almost impossible to create a list of tornado statistics for all the storms that have occurred in the United States. The main reason for this is that many tornadoes go unreported. Because they occur in remote and rural areas of the country, they are never witnessed. If they are never witnessed, they do not find their way into the meteorologists' database. Doppler radar networks can record areas of stormy weather, but unless a tornado is actually observed, no one will know about it. But given the tornadoes that have been reported, scientists are able to formulate some statistics about tornadoes' average duration, distance traveled, and wind speeds.

Wind speed is likely the hardest data to collect. Scientists have yet to develop an instrument that can record wind speeds inside a tornado, although there have been some interesting attempts. One was called TOTO, after Dorothy Gale's dog in *The Wizard of Oz*. The "*TO*table *Tornado Observatory*," or TOTO, was a 400-pound device that NOAA and University of Oklahoma researchers hoped to place in the path of a tornado. The theory was that as the twister passed over TOTO (with the researchers a safe distance away), the device would record the storm's wind speed and other statistics. Unfortunately, TOTO proved to be too cumbersome for researchers to place directly in the path of a tornado, and it was retired in 1985. By then advancements in portable Doppler units allowed observers to collect wind speed data from a safe distance as storms occurred.

As of this writing, the highest recorded wind speed for a tornado is an estimated 318 miles an hour, recorded on May 3, 1999, during the severe weather outbreak now known as the Oklahoma City/Moore tornado. But such storms are truly the exception. According to one study, fully

TOTO was a 400-pound piece of equipment that measured wind speed. It was quickly replaced once portable Doppler radar units were invented.

two-thirds of all reported tornadoes have been estimated to have wind speeds of less than 120 miles an hour.

It is somewhat easier to gauge other tornado statistics. Most tornadoes last only a few minutes; according to Roger Edwards of the Storm Prediction Center, "Most tornadoes last

The Fujita Scale

Currently, the best way to provide an assessment of a storm's power is to use the Fujita scale, developed by Professor T. Theodore Fujita of the University of Chicago. Introduced in 1971, the Fujita scale (or F-scale) became almost immediately accepted by the meteorological and engineering communities because it provides a way to assess a tornado's strength based on the *damage* caused by the storm. At present, it is science's best tool for describing and assessing the power of tornadoes.

Professor Fujita examined the damage data from a wide variety of storms and the relative strengths of different types of construction, such as wooden houses versus brick houses. He assigned numbers from zero to five to historical storms based on the amount of destruction caused, with an F-0 storm being a weak tornado of 40 to 72 miles per hour and an F-5 being from 261 to 318 miles per hour. According to the F-scale, an F-0 storm would cause light damage, such as breaking tree limbs and damaging chimneys and signboards. An F-5 would cause incredible damage, such as lifting strong frame houses off their foundations and carrying them considerable distances before ripping them apart and propelling automobile-sized items through the air for a hundred yards or more.

While the F-scale is now widely used by news reports as well as official damage assessments, it is not perfect. Meteorologist J.R. McDonald's article "T. Theodore Fujita: His Contribution to Tornado Knowledge Through Damage Documentation and the Fujita Scale" in the *Bulletin of the American Meteorological Society*'s January 2001 issue, points out:

> The F scale has not been without limitations and controversy. Early on, Fujita acknowledged that the original damage descriptions for each category do not recognize differences in construction quality. If a barn or a manufactured house is destroyed, the tornado may be assigned a more intense F scale rating than if it passes over a well-constructed building and causes little or no damage. Another limitation on the F scale concept appears when there are no damage indicators in the storm path. A storm passing over open country could be rated at a classification lower than actual intensity.

less than ten minutes," but some can last up to "more than an hour."[30] Average forward speed is approximately twenty miles an hour, and average path traveled, according to researchers, is "about one mile long."[31]

The record for longest tornado duration seems to be impossible to determine. The National Weather Service lists twenty-eight tornadoes that have traveled more than a hundred miles, although some researchers argue that given what is now known about thunderstorms, supercells, and tornadogenesis, such great distances are unlikely. Damage paths of such lengths are likely due to multiple tornadoes that are subsequently reported as a single event.

Professor T. Theodore Fujita works in his lab with a tornado simulator. Professor Fujita developed the Fujita scale, a method of assessing a tornado's strength.

For example, suppose a tornado touched down in Ohio in 1930. Researchers might find accounts of the storm in local newspapers or magazines. If a tornado was also reported in neighboring eastern Indiana or northern Kentucky on the same day, the researcher might assume that the tornado in Ohio had first touched down in Indiana, then passed through Kentucky, and then into Ohio, thus attributing to this storm a path of perhaps more than a hundred miles. In fact, while the reported tornadoes may have been spawned from the same supercell, it is more likely that each report recorded a separate tornado.

Similarly, it is difficult to pinpoint an average tornado path width or to award one tornado the distinction of having the widest path. Once again, researchers are hampered by eyewitness accounts or a lack of eyewitnesses altogether. The National Weather Service records list the May 31, 1985, tornado that hit Pennsylvania as having the greatest width, of 1.9 miles across. But it may be that no one actually saw it, since the tornado traveled mostly across Moshannon State Forest; and it may be that the storm was actually wider than 1.9 miles, with some records suggesting it was as wide as 2.2 miles across. The width estimates are based on the damage the storm left behind.

The Moshannon State Park tornado is an example of how investigators can reconstruct events. Even if no one is around to see a storm, researchers and scientists can now determine a great deal of information from the tornado's path of damage and destruction. However, regardless of which tornado was the widest, had the highest wind speed, or traveled the greatest distance, one remarkable storm system in 1925 spawned a tornado that experts agree traveled more than 150 miles.

One for the Record Books: The Tri-State Tornado of 1925

From 1 to 4:30 P.M., the Tri-State Tornado of March 18, 1925, ripped across Missouri, Illinois, and Indiana, heading east-northeast from Ellington, Missouri, to northeast of Princeton, Indiana. The tornado averaged a forward speed of over sixty miles an hour and destroyed schools built of wood, brick, and stone. It trapped coal miners in Illinois while the town above them was devastated and their homes were turned to splinters. It completely destroyed the towns of Gorham, Illinois, and Griffin, Indiana. Annapolis, Missouri, and Parrish, Illinois, suffered almost complete destruction, and along a twenty-mile stretch in Indiana, eighty-five farms were totally wiped out. Almost seven hundred people died across the three states. The residents had little or no warning the storm was approaching because huge clouds of dust and debris hid the funnel cloud, and because the storm approached faster than anyone could escape.

Present-day researchers believe that this storm was actually one continuous tornado. But reaching that conclusion was not an easy task. Photographs of the damage left behind were taken hours and days later, after the survivors had started to clean up some of the destruction. These efforts obscured or removed evidence of the tornado's path. Contemporary newspaper reports were sometimes based on second- and thirdhand accounts. But eyewitness reports from the survivors, combined with other evidence, led researchers to theorize that a single long-lived tornado had been the culprit.

After the tornado, news of the disaster spread slowly across the country. In 1925 there were few radio stations in the United States; the fastest way to spread news was by telegraph or telephone. But since these communications systems rely on wires (usually on poles), they are particularly vulnerable to tornadic winds even of a moderate speed. Even if Missourians had tried to alert their neighbor states, Illinois and Indiana, about this killer storm, it is unlikely the news would have reached them in time.

This photograph from 1925 illustrates damage in Griffin, Indiana, from the Tri-State Tornado. The town of Griffin was completely destroyed.

Natural disasters such as the Tri-State Tornado have contributed to the development of today's nationwide severe weather warning system. Wireless technologies such as radio, television, and cellular telephones play a large part in the communications networks that alert residents to the potential for dangerous weather. And, for most Americans, the first word of approaching weather comes from a warning issued by the National Weather Service.

Getting the Word Out

Since the 1950s the National Weather Service (NWS) has accepted the huge responsibility of keeping the United States informed about ever-changing weather conditions. Following the Palm Sunday Outbreak of killer tornadoes that swept across Illinois, Wisconsin, Michigan, Indiana, and Ohio on April 11, 1965, the NWS realized it needed to do two things better. First, it needed to improve its methods of getting severe weather information out to the public, and second, it needed to educate the public about what to do when dangerous weather approached.

Since then the NWS has been instrumental in developing public outreach programs to help alert citizens to the various attributes of severe weather. Its concerted efforts bore fruit less than ten years later when the Super Outbreak that tore through Xenia, Ohio, and caused severe damage from Alabama to West Virginia in 1974 found U.S. residents much more informed about and prepared to deal with severe weather than they had been in 1965.

This education process has included a series of information pamphlets and films that are distributed to libraries, schools, and other civic organizations. As the years have passed and science has advanced knowledge of tornadoes, the content of these documents has changed to reflect the new information and recommendations. Presenting new information can be a challenge, however. Researcher Charles Doswell writes: "Public education efforts are a major task. . . . Making changes to the safety rules, for example, has proven to be

An elementary school principal and his students practice a tornado drill in Missouri. The National Weather Service has been instrumental in helping the public learn what to do if a tornado hits.

maddeningly difficult. Myths about tornadoes survive, including myths that were once the frontiers of our science."[32]

As an example, the researchers describe a pamphlet called "Tornadoes . . . Nature's Most Violent Storms" that the NWS released in 1992. The publication attacked a popular belief that one should open windows to alleviate the pressure drops associated with tornadoes. Formerly these pressure drops were believed to play a significant part in causing buildings to "explode." Researchers comment that, as with other, older conventions that once governed people's thinking about tornado safety, "this one has been known for some time to be erroneous and possibly dangerous."[33]

The NWS continues its education efforts today and works in partnership with local emergency officials to get severe weather information to the public as soon as possible. Each local office also works with the Storm Prediction Center (SPC), formerly known as the National Severe Storms Forecast Center (NSSFC), to keep the local area informed about potential severe weather.

Watches and Warnings: The Storm Prediction Center

The SPC, a specialized unit of the NWS, provides the nation with a variety of forecasts for severe weather throughout the year. Under the direction of a lead forecaster, a team of scientists examines areas of the nation where they anticipate severe weather.

The lead forecaster's main responsibility is to issue severe thunderstorm and tornado watches as necessary. It is important to remember the difference between a severe thunderstorm or tornado watch and a warning. A "watch" means conditions are favorable for severe weather; a "warning" means severe weather is in progress or has been reported.

The lead forecaster keeps a close watch on the nation's weather, paying close attention to current and forecast weather for conditions that lead to violent thunderstorms. If a watch is issued, the lead forecaster coordinates with numerous local NWS offices in the threat areas and ensures that the watch process works smoothly. A watch alerts the public, local NWS offices, and emergency managers of the threat of severe thunderstorms and/or tornadoes during the next several hours, covering parts of one or more states. In addition to alerting the general public to a threat of severe storms, these watches also activate local SKYWARN storm spotter networks.

For example, the SPC issued this severe thunderstorm watch to area NWS offices, emergency officials, and local media on Saturday, May 30, 1998:

BULLETIN—IMMEDIATE BROADCAST REQUESTED SEVERE THUNDERSTORM WATCH NUMBER 464 STORM PREDICTION CENTER NORMAN OK

322 AM CDT [central daylight time] SAT MAY 30 1998

THE STORM PREDICTION CENTER HAS ISSUED A SEVERE
THUNDERSTORM WATCH FOR PORTIONS OF

CENTRAL AND EASTERN SOUTH DAKOTA
EXTREME NORTH CENTRAL AND NORTHEAST NEBRASKA

EFFECTIVE THIS SATURDAY MORNING FROM 400 AM UNTIL
1000 AM CDT.
HAIL TO 2 INCHES IN DIAMETER . . . THUNDERSTORM WIND
GUSTS TO 70 MPH . . . AND DANGEROUS LIGHTNING ARE
POSSIBLE IN THESE AREAS.
THE SEVERE THUNDERSTORM WATCH AREA IS ALONG AND
70 STATUTE MILES NORTH AND SOUTH OF A LINE FROM 20
MILES WEST SOUTHWEST OF PHILIP SOUTH DAKOTA TO 10
MILES EAST OF SIOUX FALLS SOUTH DAKOTA.
REMEMBER . . . A SEVERE THUNDERSTORM WATCH MEANS
CONDITIONS ARE FAVORABLE FOR SEVERE THUNDERSTORMS
IN AND CLOSE TO THE WATCH AREA.
PERSONS IN THESE AREAS SHOULD BE ON THE LOOKOUT
FOR THREATENING WEATHER CONDITIONS AND LISTEN FOR
LATER STATEMENTS AND POSSIBLE WARNINGS.[34]

Throughout the early morning of May 30, the SPC continued to monitor the situation and issued further updates on the situation throughout the day.

Once a watch is issued, the SPC may modify it by focusing the watch on a smaller area or upgrade the watch to a warning if SKYWARN members or emergency officials spot and report a tornado. Alternatively, the watch may be canceled altogether if the system moves out of the watch area or dissipates.

As severe weather approaches, the area's emergency officials alert the residents in many ways. Local radio and television broadcasts are interrupted with severe weather alerts and bulletins; sometimes television stations insert a "crawl" (a small area, usually in red, across the bottom of the screen with text of the alert) with an attention-getting series of tones.

The Storm Prediction Center monitors storm conditions such as this anvil head storm cloud. A storm or tornado watch or warning is then issued if severe weather develops.

Police and fire personnel may drive through neighborhoods in the line of the storm, broadcasting alerts over loudspeakers. Other areas have tornado sirens that are activated when an alert is received. However, sometimes the best-laid plans of all emergency officials are insufficient to alert everyone in time. This was the case when a tornado bore down on Spencer, South Dakota, in 1998.

Spencer, South Dakota, May 30, 1998

The small town of Spencer, roughly halfway between the cities of Mitchell and Sioux Falls in eastern South Dakota, was a farming community of about three hundred residents on the afternoon of Saturday, May 30, 1998. Within twenty-four hours, a mile-wide tornado ripped through the town, killing six and injuring half of the town's residents.

The SPC had watched the conditions become more and more favorable for tornadogenesis throughout Saturday. The severe thunderstorm watch issued by the SPC that appears above covered the area surrounding and including Spencer, and as Saturday, May 30, continued, the SPC noted that the atmosphere was becoming more unstable. One alert that afternoon mentioned that "wind profiles will also remain favorable for supercell development" and that as the situation continued to develop, the eastern South Dakota area was "being considered for a tornado watch in the next 1–2 hours."[35]

A tornado watch was issued for eastern South Dakota at 3:50 P.M. central daylight time, lasting until 10 P.M. The SPC released a further update after 8 P.M., extending the watch until 3 A.M. Sunday, calling it "a particularly dangerous situation with the possibility of very damaging tornadoes."[36] The tornado struck Spencer at 8:45 P.M.

The town had lost electricity before the tornado hit, so the tornado warning sirens did not activate. But, as South Dakota governor Bill Janklow said, "Look at this town. A siren wouldn't have made a difference. The fact is we are lucky we didn't have 200 killed in this devastation. That was a miracle."[37]

Spencer residents had taken varying amounts of precautions as the severe weather had approached. Some were prepared; twelve residents of an apartment building had developed their own tornado plan and designated a storeroom beneath a staircase as their shelter. All twelve survived. Others had not paid attention to the weather alerts until the electricity went off. By then, for some it was too late to take shelter. One senior citizen, recovering from surgery, rode out the tornado in her recliner, unable to move. She was unhurt. But another elderly woman died when she was swept from her second-floor apartment by the storm's fury.

The residents of Spencer gathered on June 1, the Monday following the tornado, and heard Governor Janklow insist that the town would be rebuilt. Many were willing to stay; others were unsure where they would live. The owner of the town's only gas station and convenience store had watched the tornado blow away his business in a few seconds. He said, "I really don't know what to do. I am waiting to see. . . . I want to stay, but right now I don't know."[38]

What Next?

For a few days in 1998, the nation watched and listened to what had happened to Spencer, South Dakota. Soon, however, other events and demands of everyday life turned the average citizen's attention away from Spencer, while the residents there tried to rebuild their lives. The victims of tornadoes across the country, and indeed all over the world, have the same initial reaction as the convenience store owner in Spencer: "I really don't know what to do." Generosity, communication, and prior planning often dictate the actions of friends, neighbors, and a community following such an event. All three are important in the days, weeks, and months after a tornado strikes.

Aftermath

Although a tornado can hit with tremendous ferocity, the storm itself generally does not stay long over a particular area. A tornado can arrive, strike, and depart in only a matter of minutes. Once the severe weather has passed, residents must deal with its aftermath; this includes attending to the pressing needs of family, friends, neighbors, and often complete strangers.

First on the Scene: Friends and Neighbors

In many stories of the aftermaths of tornadoes, the first people to arrive on the scene are friends and neighbors whose lives, and perhaps property, had been spared by the storm's fury. In the farming areas of the Great Plains, residents may travel several miles in the tornado's path to see what assistance can be rendered. The willingness to embark on such journeys was particularly important in the days before widespread communications networks. Since news of a disaster often did not reach government emergency officials promptly, tornado survivors frequently had to fend for themselves for days before outside help arrived.

In Spencer, South Dakota, residents who had survived the storm emerged from their homes not only to see what had happened to their own belongings but to check on their neighbors. Bob and Rozella Loon had been visiting friends in Spencer and took shelter in the home's basement as the tornado passed. After the storm passed, Bob Loon said they "climbed over trees and power poles [and] Rozella helped older folks out of the wreckage"[39] as they worked their way to the emergency command post on the edge of town.

In the immediate aftermath of a storm, people may be more concerned about their neighbors than they are about themselves. When a series of unexpected tornadoes hit the farming communities of the southern Ontario province in Canada on April 20, 1996, many families lost barns, sheds, chicken coops, and other farm buildings. Others saw their homes damaged or destroyed. Barb Hanley had survived the storm, and although she discovered that her bedroom wall and roof were gone, her first thoughts were about her neighbor, Ernie Plant, who was almost eighty years old. She looked toward his

Family, friends, and neighbors will rush to console and help victims of tornadoes and are usually on the scene before rescue and disaster personnel.

house and saw nothing there. Plant's neighbors to the east, Mike Boivin and his daughter Michelle, climbed from the rubble of their home and also thought of Ernie. They found Plant out in a field. He later said that before the storm, "I had just put a can of soup in a pot and put it on the stove. . . . I didn't know a thing about it until it hit."[40] The older man had no idea how he got out into the field. Miraculously, he only had a few bumps and bruises.

The debris left behind from Ernie Plant's house was similar to debris left behind after any tornado. Following the Oklahoma City/Moore tornado of May 3, 1999, Charles A. Doswell of the National Severe Storms Laboratory spent some time studying the storm's aftermath. He was struck by the amount of debris in the residential areas, as well as how the area affected his sense of smell.

> I am acutely aware by now of the smell of a tornado track. This musty smell is hard to describe and I don't know its origins. Perhaps it's the smell of wet ceiling tiles, paper, rotting food, and insulation. . . . Everywhere, the rubble has a monotonous sameness: shattered framing lumber, shards of insulation, broken glass, drywall boards, shelving units, refrigerators, shingles, collapsed brick veneer, jagged leafless branches from trees. . . . I'm also struck by the huge amount of "stuff" that fills the rubble piles: toys, Christmas decorations, magazines, vases and lamps (mostly broken), televisions, boxes of baseball cards, food from pantries (jars of pickles, bags of chips, cans of beans, spice bottles), stuffed animals, video cassettes, compact discs, photos in frames, decorative items of all sorts and descriptions. . . . These, after all, are real people, with "stuff" that looks a lot like my "stuff."[41]

Eventually, as news of the storm spreads, others make their way to the scene to offer aid. When the tornado hit Spencer, the Storm Prediction Center (SPC) had several crews in the area, mostly by chance. The team of Keith Brown and Martin

Lisius had been amazed by the storm's power as they had studied it when it passed to the east of them, but they did not find out about what had happened to Spencer until later that evening. When they tried to visit Spencer the next day to see if they could help, they discovered that

> Highway 38 was busy on the south side of town as a media camp had been established. All roads to Spencer were blocked by order of the McCook County Sheriff. Large trees were stripped clean of branches and leaves, [and] a farmer placed dead cattle into a truck using a front-end loader. The sounds of earth-moving equipment drifted in the wind. We saw a car in a tree, farmsteads destroyed, a toppled grain elevator, and what looked like a bombed-out town. We measured the tornado's path at .8 mile wide at Highway 38. Northwest of town, we estimated damage along an east-west section road at 1.5 miles long. The damage was incredible.[42]

Lisius and Brown discovered that the town had already started to rebuild and the emergency officials had matters well in hand in the aftermath of the tornado. It was now time to let those trained in emergencies and disasters take over.

Emergency Officials Respond

After severe weather strikes, and sometimes while the event is still in progress, emergency officials arrive on the scene. Police officers, fire department personnel, emergency medical technicians, doctors, nurses, and volunteers may all find themselves wishing to help. Immediately after the storm passes, the emergency response officials must determine what needs to be done.

Many communities have an emergency response plan that details which officials are responsible for what duties in the aftermath of a tornado. The plan may be a simple guide to the neighborhoods of the community, showing which buildings are home to residents who may need assistance, such as those

An injured tornado victim is helped from the rubble in Moore, Oklahoma. Emergency officials have disaster plans in place so they can respond quickly and efficiently to help the victims.

who are elderly or have disabilities, and who may not have been able to reach shelter. Other plans have more detailed information showing such important locations as shutoff valves for water and natural gas supplies or electrical systems.

In any case, whether a plan exists or not, emergency officials have to make a number of decisions quickly following a tornado. They need to assess if there are any situations that threaten immediate danger to the community. Individuals who are trapped in homes shattered by the storm will need the first response of emergency officials, while those who have survived with minor injuries await attention.

As reports come in to the emergency officials, they need to prioritize them by their potential danger to residents. In the case of large-scale damage and destruction, it is important for emergency officials to know how to react. Hospitals and emergency rooms set up priority treatment schedules called triage, in which the most life-threatening injuries receive immediate care. Those with lesser injuries, such as Ernie Plant of Ontario, may be hospitalized briefly for observation but will soon be allowed to go home to start to rebuild their lives.

Larger Towns, Larger Disasters

Tornadoes do not only hit rural areas. Cities as large as Tulsa and Oklahoma City, Oklahoma, have seen dozens of tornadoes in their immediate areas over the last thirty years. Meteorologist Gary England of KWTV in Oklahoma City writes in *Weathering the Storm: Tornadoes, Television, and Turmoil* that in one memorable year, "seven twisters touched down within a fifteen-mile radius of the television station." And as cities continue to grow in population, it remains only a matter of time before a major metropolitan area gets a direct hit from a major tornado.

A tornado on May 3, 1999, did not hit Oklahoma City's densely built downtown directly, but it came very close. In its path were several of the city's suburbs and neighboring communities, and it devastated many of them, including the town of Moore, Oklahoma. By the time the Oklahoma City/Moore tornado dissipated, it had destroyed almost two thousand homes and damaged twenty-five hundred more, resulting in over $1 billion in damage. The SPC's Daniel McCarthy and Joseph T. Schaefer's "Twisters Go Urban," in the March/April 2000 issue of *Weatherwise*, describe the tornado's destruction through the Eastlake Estates subdivision in southwest Oklahoma City:

> As it hit the subdivision, [the tornado] caus[ed] widespread demolition. Entire rows of homes were virtually flattened into piles of rubble, and adjacent homes were cleaned off their foundations, leaving only the concrete slabs. A 600-unit apartment complex was destroyed with one of the apartment buildings flattened. All that is left today is the swimming pool and its surrounding fence.

The Recovery Begins

But many survivors, like Ernie Plant, have no home left standing. Some of the victims of a tornado truly have nothing with which to rebuild their lives. In the aftermath of the Oklahoma City/Moore tornado, hundreds of people "left with literally nothing more than the clothes on their backs"[43] turned to the

A tornado touches down in the middle of a city. Tornadoes can happen anywhere the atmospheric conditions are right.

But it was in the communities of Bridge Creek and Moore that the tornado did its heaviest destruction. More than two hundred mobile homes and houses in Bridge Creek were totally destroyed or damaged, killing twelve people; in Moore two elementary schools were destroyed and a high school was heavily damaged. In all, thirty-eight people lost their lives in this monster storm and over six hundred were injured.

generosity of the United States Air Force at nearby Tinker Air Force Base. Reservists from the Air Force Reserve Command's 507th Air Refueling Wing and the 513th Air Control Group, along with their active-duty counterparts, hurriedly put together a makeshift hotel for some of the victims. They set up a food kitchen and more than three hundred cots in a hangar that usually houses a giant KC-135 refueling tanker airplane. The base's search-and-rescue teams and medical technicians joined other emergency officials to work in the tornado's wake.

One medical technician, Senior Airman Scott Branscum of Moore, said, "I saw the twister go past my home. It was only 150 yards away. The noise sounded like a jet engine revving up, only it just kept getting louder and louder. My wife and I had our children in the bathtub. Our home had some damage, but some of my neighbors' homes just aren't there now." He drove to the base through streets jammed with debris and stopped to help when he could. One woman in a retirement home "was buried under five feet of rubble," said Branscum, who worked frantically with several other strangers to dig the woman out. "A wall had fallen on top of her," he said. "But by some miracle her walker, which had fallen on top of her, saved the woman. It formed a brace and kept everything from crushing her. She had a dislocated shoulder and cuts, but she was alright,"[44] he said.

Occasionally, emergency officials arrive on the scene and find that a building's occupants are in better shape than they had hoped. In the wake of the southern Ontario tornadoes, Dave and Sue Comber were surprised to find the local fire department arrive at their home, but perhaps the firefighters were even more surprised. Their house, located on forested land well back from the main road, was damaged, but the Combers were unhurt. After the storm, Sue, a diabetic, needed to eat to have her medicine work properly. Sue said, "We're sitting here and eating like nothing has happened, and the boys of the Chatsworth Fire Department came roaring in. They were here within fifteen minutes. . . . [T]hey came down here not knowing whether there was a house here or whether we were buried under the debris or what."[45]

The Chatsworth firefighters undoubtedly were prepared for the worst at the Combers' house. Often in the wake of a tornado, firefighters and emergency personnel have to deal with downed electrical power lines that still have electricity flowing through them and therefore are extremely dangerous. Sparks from downed lines can start fires among debris or ignite natural gas leaking from ruptured underground pipelines. However, in many cases, when a tornado snaps power lines, the electric company's emergency circuit breakers shut down the power flow. This prevents any other lines from presenting a hazard for rescue workers.

Once the immediate emergencies have been handled, the emergency officials, residents, neighbors, volunteers, and strangers can turn to less-pressing needs. In farming communities, this often includes taking inventory of the livestock to see how many have survived the tornado. Cattle are occasionally killed by the force of the storm when they are picked up and dropped by the winds or are crushed when a barn collapses on top of them. But sometimes they survive by the oddest circumstances. In one instance, a calf was found hanging in a tree. The owner said, "It had a dislocated back leg, but they just sawed the branches off the tree and it plopped to the ground, and away it went."[46] Such positive events make the recovery process just a little bit easier for all involved.

Spencer's Recovery: May 30 and Beyond

For the residents of Spencer, South Dakota, who surveyed the damage from the May 30, 1998, tornado, recovery meant facing hard choices about not only the future of their town's homes and businesses, but of the future of the town itself. Despite Governor Bill Janklow's insistence that Spencer would be rebuilt, many local residents had their doubts. The tornado had destroyed all of the town's businesses, and more than half of the homes were damaged. But as news of the town's situation spread, help started coming

Tornadoes and Mobile Homes

Scientists who use the Fujita scale to estimate the relative strengths of tornadoes encounter a dilemma when a storm has inflicted damage on a mobile home or a community of mobile homes. As these structures are more lightly built than more traditional homes, they often

Mobile homes and their occupants are particularly at risk in a tornado.

suffer greater damage than other structures. For example, the 1999 Oklahoma City/Moore tornado removed the roofs of frame houses (which would lead to the storm being classified as an F-2), but also produced F-4 damage as it swept homes from their concrete slabs, as well as F-5 damage when it destroyed hundreds of mobile homes in several areas.

While it is true that mobile homes suffer more damage in comparison to traditional homes, it is only a myth that tornadoes are "attracted" to mobile homes or deliberately target them. The homes' less sturdy construction is the only reason they suffer greater losses.

Additionally, there tend to be more injuries to mobile home residents when tornadoes strike. One reason is that these structures rarely have a place where residents can take shelter, such as a basement or a sturdy interior room. In "Billion-Dollar Twister," an article in *Scientific American*, meteorologist Robert Henson of the University Corporation for Atmospheric Research elaborates:

> Mobile homes tend to be unsafe at any tornadic speed; nearly half of all tornado deaths since 1975 have occurred in them. Yet few mobile-home residents have access to shelters. One recent damage survey led by Thomas W. Schmidlin of Kent State University hints that for tornadoes of F2 to F3 intensity, it could be safer for mobile-home residents to stay in parked cars than to remain in their homes. The cars, being more aerodynamic, appear far less likely than mobile homes to tip over and disintegrate when lashed by the wind. In an F4 or F5, of course, all bets are off.

in from not only across the state, but from across the country as well.

After a natural disaster such as a tornado, local elected officials have many options for assistance at their disposal. In the case of the Spencer tornado, local officials contacted the governor's office, and after touring the site, Governor Janklow declared it a disaster area. This declaration sets a number of wheels in motion, at the state and the federal level. All states have money available in disaster relief funds, which can be distributed to the affected communities. In addition, a branch of the United States government called the Federal Emergency Management Agency (FEMA) deals solely with disasters. After the Spencer tornado, Governor Janklow contacted FEMA to see if the area qualified for federal disaster assistance.

With the aid of federal and state funds, the town began to slowly return to life. The residents of Spencer began rebuilding homes and businesses almost immediately after the storm passed. Vice President Al Gore visited Spencer a week after the tornado, and promised federal aid. FEMA originally estimated that $376,663 would cover the portion of rebuilding projects not covered by insurance, but by May of the following year, FEMA had allocated nearly $2 million in disaster aid.

In the meantime, other concerned individuals and groups offered assistance. Disasters often bring out the generous nature in people, and contributions to fund-raising efforts and charities begin to flow in almost as soon as the tornado has passed.

The Generosity of Strangers: Charities

After the Spencer tornado, Governor Janklow established a state-run fund to gather donations from fellow South Dakotans specifically for Spencer's recovery. Many state residents sent checks or called the toll-free telephone number to pledge support, and by the first anniversary of the tornado (May 30, 1999), the fund had collected over $1 million in contributions.

The Sioux Falls newspaper documented other recovery contributions:

The American Red Cross established a disaster relief center in Texas (above) after a tornado slammed through Jarrell in May 1997. The Red Cross also sent meal trucks to Arkansas (right) after a tornado hit Arkadelphia in March 1997.

Sioux Falls radio stations are holding fund-raisers for Spencer tornado victims this week. KIKN, 100.5, will begin a marathon broadcast starting at 5:30 A.M. today and continuing until contributions reach $10,050. The station will auction various country music collectibles and a car during the broadcast. The station also has a drop-off box for donated items at its office. . . . Barnes and Noble will donate to the relief fund a percentage of store sales from 9 A.M. to 11 P.M. on Saturday. . . . Officials from ShopKo Stores, Inc. [have donated] $5,000 for tornado victims. The donation was made on behalf of the company's stores in Mitchell and Sioux Falls. . . . The Gateway Foundation has established a fund to assist residents of Spencer. The foundation will match contributions by Gateway [Computers] employees in Sioux Falls, Vermillion and North Sioux City.[47]

In addition to private businesses such as radio stations, banks, and businesses, other organizations rushed in to help the victims in Spencer. Two nationwide charities, the American Red Cross and the Salvation Army, assisted state, local, and federal relief efforts by setting up temporary shelters for disaster victims. They collected food, clothing, and money for the survivors and helped them to get in touch with family and friends across the country.

On the first anniversary of the storm, South Dakota Public Broadcasting compiled a list of aid and contributions that had been delivered to Spencer. In addition to the nearly $2 million from FEMA and the over $1 million in the Governor's Fund, there was $1 million from the U.S. government through Community Development Block Grant Funds, and $2,171,298 in "Individual Assistance." The "Individual Assistance" category included $612,402 that had been donated by July 28, 1998, nearly half of which was from the Spencer Area Recovery and Interfaith Network, a network of churches throughout South Dakota.

Residents of other states have been equally generous in helping fellow Americans to recover from tornadoes. For example, after tornadoes struck the Owensboro, Kentucky, area on January 3, 2000, donations came in from across Kentucky and from citizens in neighboring Ohio and Indiana as well. In addition, funds from FEMA, the Red Cross, and other agencies helped the community recovery efforts. For example, the Big Rivers chapter of the American Red Cross raised $707,000 in donations raised locally on disaster services and vouchers to help victims with immediate needs:

> Most of that money, $537,000, came from a telethon sponsored by [television station] NBC 14-WFIE in Evansville [Indiana]. The money went quickly, as Red Cross volunteers dished up 43,319 meals at four feeding

sites and 10 mobile units. The agency distributed 12,000
cleaning kits, operated an emergency shelter . . . for seven
days and completed 641 medical, service and support vis-
its. When the initial phase of the tragedy had passed,
nearly 600 families had been touched by the Red Cross.[48]

Interestingly, a year after the tornado, some of the funds do-
nated during the Owensboro aftermath remained unspent. The
Owensboro-Daviess County Tornado Relief Fund had raised
about $158,000, and by the first anniversary of the tornado, they
had committed nearly $100,000 to repair tornado-damaged
homes and to complete their last few projects. However, the
fund still had $110,799, thanks to "resourceful investing," ac-
cording to City Manager Ron Payne, with any funds left over set
aside for any future disaster needs. Payne said, "There's no way
we can return that money, so we're just going to sit on it and use
it for any future disasters in the community."[49]

Such farsighted planning on the part of community leaders
ensures that the Owensboro area may be able to help even
more families if another disaster strikes. However, many individuals choose not to rely on the chance that local or federal
funds will become available during or after a disaster. They
decide to buy private insurance policies that are intended to
reimburse them for their losses.

Insurance Against the Unknown and Unexpected

As early as 1884, farmers in Iowa were able to buy insurance
against tornado and wind damage. This was at a time when
weather forecasting was very primitive, and the U.S. Weather
Bureau (the forerunner of the National Weather Service)
would not allow weather observers to use the word "tornado"
in their reports. Today many homeowners' policies have some
protection against natural disasters, and many insurance com-
panies can provide insurance policies specifically against
losses associated with tornadoes.

In the aftermath of tornadoes, policyholders file claims to
try to recover their losses. After the Spencer tornado, 10,900

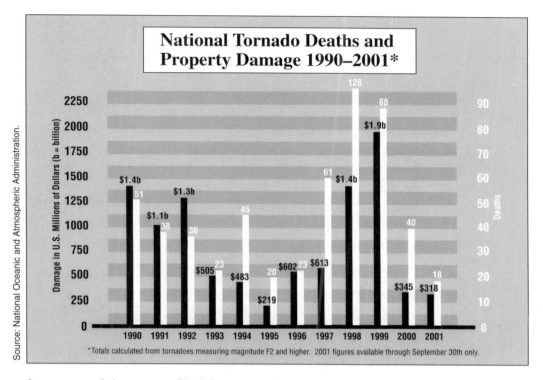

National Tornado Deaths and Property Damage 1990–2001*

Source: National Oceanic and Atmospheric Administration.

Damage in U.S. Millions of Dollars (b = billion)

Deaths

*Totals calculated from tornadoes measuring magnitude F2 and higher. 2001 figures available through September 30th only.

insurance claims were filed for storm damage in Spencer and the surrounding five-county area, totaling $25 million. After a larger-scale disaster, claims totals can go far higher. A few days after the tornado outbreak of May 3, 1999, which stretched across Oklahoma and Kansas and included the Oklahoma City/Moore tornado, the Insurance Information Institute estimated that insured losses "could exceed $500 million."[50]

Insurance policies can provide a certain sense of peace of mind because the policyholders know that they will be reimbursed for the cash value of possessions and property lost in a disaster. Insurance investigators are authorized to literally write a check on the spot when they can determine that a policyholder's claim is legitimate, but some insurance claims drag on for weeks, months, or even years. For example, in the event of disagreement between an insurance company's claims investigator and a policyholder over whether losses are directly related to the tornado, the policyholder may have to furnish evidence that the losses were directly related to the tornado. In such circumstances, it may seem to the parties that the aftermath of the tornado will never end.

In the aftermath of the Owensboro tornado, Steve Flener, district coordinator for the United Methodist Council on Relief, said, "There are some cases where insurance gave a check that night . . . but there are others who still have not received checks as of last month. . . . Some of the needs that insurance is not taking care of (include) the repair work. We've found that (some) insurance . . . pays off the mortgage but doesn't pay for any repair work on the house."[51]

A tornado completely leveled this Oklahoma neighborhood in May 1999. The Insurance Information Institute estimated insured losses at $500 million for this disaster which stretched across Oklahoma and Kansas.

In other cases, policyholders may discover that what is a disaster for them does not meet official definitions of "disaster." In July 2001 a tornado that started as a waterspout came ashore in coastal South Carolina. But as damage was estimated at only $9 million, the area did not qualify as a disaster area, leaving many policyholders with less reimbursement than they hoped. Some who rebuilt their homes or businesses faced unexpected expenses for years to come in the aftermath of this rare coastal tornado.

When Does the Aftermath End?

Traumatic events such as tornadoes have been known to leave a deep and lasting impression on both the survivors and those who responded to the event. How they deal with the feelings associated with the tornado and its aftermath may be an important factor in how the individual faces the future.

A tornado may cause damage only in a small area, or it may bring widespread destruction. Each person has a different response to such emergencies. Some people are able to rebuild and continue their lives as before, learning valuable lessons about tornado survival that may become important in the future. Some people seek counseling to deal with the experience, such as Stephanie Wilson of Owensboro, Kentucky, who lived through the January 3, 2000, tornado and said, "I can't stand still on Fridays when they test the tornado siren. I can't stand to hear it."[52] Still others decide to study the event in great detail to learn what can be done to prepare their community for the next tornado, in hopes of minimizing the storm's effects and its aftermath.

5

What Can Be Done?: A Glimpse into the Future

A tornado forms, touches down, carves a swath of destruction across the landscape, and disappears into the clouds from which it came. The scientists, witnesses, and survivors may marvel at the storm's power and curse its destructive nature, but each may silently wonder what can be done to deal with the next tornadic outbreak. Such musings have led some people to develop ideas about how to better prepare for and forecast tornadoes and have led others to wonder if they can be removed as a threat altogether.

"Everybody Talks About the Weather"

Removing tornadoes from the landscape, or, at least, diminishing their ability to threaten lives and property, is currently only possible in the world of science fiction. Science is still attempting to understand how tornadoes form and how they can be forecast. Although the saying "Everybody talks about the weather, but nobody does anything about it" is still true, such limitations on scientific knowledge have not prevented individuals from theorizing about how tornadoes could be controlled or eliminated.

In some cases, these ideas have touched on the amount of moisture present in a supercell thunderstorm. One suggestion involves "seeding clouds to alter updrafts and precipitation."[53] Since it is possible to "seed" clouds with a chemical such as silver iodide, in the hopes that the clouds will release their moisture as rain, some researchers have suggested that seeding thunderstorm supercells ought to discourage tornadogenesis, because the clouds' energy would be dissipated as soon as the moisture began to fall.

However, the scientific community is skeptical about the feasibility of such a plan. Thomas P. Grazulis of the Tornado Project says that cloud seeding "may produce flash floods that are more costly than the tornado itself."[54] Roger Edwards of the Storm Prediction Center (SPC) contends that "because the effects of seeding are impossible to prove or disprove, there is a great deal of controversy in meteorology about whether it works, and if so, under what conditions, and to what extent."[55]

As meteorologists continue to study under what conditions tornadoes form and exist, and as they learn more about their destructive potential, they remain reluctant to add anything to the atmospheric mixture that could change a storm's nature. Thus a proposal to introduce explosives to supercells

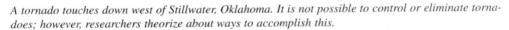

A tornado touches down west of Stillwater, Oklahoma. It is not possible to control or eliminate tornadoes; however, researchers theorize about ways to accomplish this.

is widely regarded not only as a bad idea but as potentially more destructive than any tornadoes the supercells might have spawned.

A Technological Dead End

Occasionally scientists hear proposals to destroy existing tornadoes by means of explosives, including using thermonuclear devices such as hydrogen bombs. If meteorologists are dubious about the feasibility of cloud seeding, they are definitely opposed to using explosives in any shape or form. Experts say that any device, such as a hydrogen bomb, that would be powerful enough to have any "significant impact" on a tornado would probably "be even more destructive"[56] to the landscape than the storm itself. Thomas Grazulis feels that a nuclear explosion within a tornadic supercell would add so much heat energy that it "could make the storm stronger rather than weaker."[57] Perhaps Roger Edwards of the SPC puts the objections most succinctly: "In short—bad idea!"[58]

Thus, given the current state of scientific knowledge about tornadoes, weather professionals feel that there is no way to control, modify, or destroy these storms in order to save property and lives from their effects. The University of Oklahoma's Howard Bluestein admits:

> We cannot really hope to attempt to modify tornadoes until we learn precisely how they form. . . . If we were to prevent the tornado's parent storm from forming, farmland might be deprived of much-needed rain. We might succeed in preventing tornadoes, but the consequences might be to increase the size and frequency of large hail or the intensity of surface straight-line winds (as opposed to winds in tornadoes) or the amount of rain, the latter of which could lead to flooding. In other words, the overall damage and injury from non-tornado phenomena might be worse than those caused by tornadoes themselves.[59]

Therefore, instead of dealing with weather modification theories, suggestions, and ideas, scientists are now concentrating on dealing with the next potentially severe tornadic outbreak. In order to further their knowledge of tornadoes, these professionals work on two parallel tracks. One track involves existing technology, and the other involves technology that only exists on today's drawing boards.

Using Existing Technology

In the aftermath of the Spencer, South Dakota, tornado, scientists, engineers, elected officials, and local citizens began to study the event and to find out what could be done to prevent, or at least minimize, any effects from future tornadoes. Governor Janklow promised that the area siren system, which had failed to alert residents at the critical time, would be upgraded as part of a statewide improvement plan and would include a battery backup to ensure timely alerts. The existing technology needed to be enhanced to protect Spencer's citizens in the future.

Spencer and small communities similar to it also benefit from the current use of Doppler radar systems across the United States. The nation is now blanketed by Doppler radar coverage, as the National Weather Service (NWS) has completed

The first Doppler radar station (top) was built in Oklahoma in 1973. A Doppler radar screen (bottom) displays a squall line.

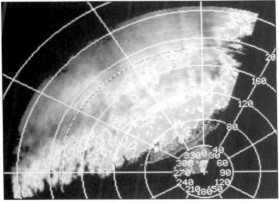

the network's installation and the training needed for its personnel to properly interpret the radar data. However, Doppler radar is only one link in the chain of people and technology needed to protect lives and property. Canadian tornado researchers and storm chasers Jerrine and Arjen Verkaik believe that technology is only part of the story:

> After damaging tornadoes strike, there are usually calls for better alert systems—more bells and whistles (sirens, public address systems, better technology). Even if there were Doppler radar on every corner, the weather office could not alert people to dangerous weather without much better communication . . . and public awareness about severe weather. . . . Even if every town had a tornado siren . . . the best warning you could expect is twenty minutes.[60]

Twenty minutes may not seem like a very long time, but that is double the amount of warning time meteorologists were able to give just a few years ago. In the 1970s Don Burgess of the National Severe Storms Laboratory (NSSL) studied the Doppler radar signatures of thirty-seven mesocyclones that produced twenty-three tornadoes. He discovered that the average elapsed time between the appearance of the mesocyclone and the touchdown of a tornado was thirty-six minutes. Relying only on visual sighting of a tornado touchdown before issuing a tornado warning through the NWS gives a lead time of only about two minutes. As university and government researchers came to realize the great potential for improved lead time through the use of Doppler radar, Burgess's discoveries added weight to the arguments in favor of a nationwide Doppler network.

This system now works so well that in some cases citizens have more than enough time to take shelter from an approaching tornado. During the outbreak of May 5, 1999, an emergency management expert "suggested that people south of Oklahoma City had so much warning that they could have dug a storm shelter in time for the tornado's passage."[61] The key to having plenty of warning was in the television media; in the Oklahoma City area, television stations have taken advantage of each advance in meteorology to keep their viewers informed.

Keeping Informed and Being Prepared

While Arjen and Jerrine Verkaik believe that "the best warning you can have comes from keeping your eyes on the sky,"[62] it always helps to have someone else doing it as well. Professional severe weather watchers and meteorologists who work for radio and television stations understand the skies and the technology needed to help the average citizen prepare for dangerous weather.

These professionals, such as Oklahoma City's Gary England at KWTV, take their education roles very seriously. For the last twenty years, England has presented his "Those Terrible Twisters" multimedia shows across Oklahoma, educating over 250,000 people about the storms. He says:

> Throughout the years the Terrible Twisters show has evolved into a major production. It includes a four-hundred-square-foot video screen with first-rate projection systems and backups, a powerful sound system with backup, strobe lights, and storm video guaranteed to entertain and thrill all those in attendance.[63]

Such presentations undoubtedly helped those who lived in the path of the May 5, 1999, tornadoes to know how to recognize tornadoes and what to do when they threaten the area. The Oklahoma City television stations have been pioneers in nowcasting, which allows their weather professionals to immediately alert their viewers to dangerous weather. They use not only the latest in Doppler radar systems, but have adapted other current technology to aid their viewers. One innovation is the towercam, which is a video camera atop a thousand-foot-tall transmission tower. The towercams broadcast live pictures of approaching storms and were invaluable during

Network and cable news organizations such as CNN play a crucial role in keeping the public informed of approaching storm conditions. Many have their own weather professionals and equipment.

the May 5 outbreak. Also, the stations employ storm chasers who work with remote cameras from both cars and helicopters to allow them to "pinpoint severe storm activity to the street location and to get the live pictures on the air."[64]

Nowcasting is important, but may not reach all the citizens in the storm's path. Today many people rely on cable television or satellite broadcasts for their entertainment and may not hear or see important local information carried by traditional "over the air" stations. Keeping these viewers informed remains a challenge for broadcasters. Local cable outlets can switch or modify programming if necessary, but the current technology allows no such accommodation for satellite systems. The key, as always, will be for citizens to remain alert to changing weather conditions.

Since the weather is constantly changing, meteorologists strive to keep abreast of what lies ahead. Researchers are attempting to improve current technologies and create new ones that will allow better understanding of complex weather patterns, storm formation, and storm behavior. Some technology is being tested today, including the next generation of radar warning systems.

The Next Generation of Forecasting

In 1999 the next generation of tornado forecasting technology was installed for testing in a weather station in northern Georgia. The Next Generation Warning Decision Support System (NG-WDSS) is a product of the NSSL and researchers from Georgia Tech University. The key to this new system is its ability to make better use of the information that the forecasters receive from Doppler radar and other sources. According to the National Oceanic and Atmospheric Administration (NOAA),

> NG-WDSS provides a set of tools that help forecasters make more efficient, effective and timely decisions on warning the public of tornadoes, severe thunderstorms and flash floods. The system includes advanced image processing, artificial intelligence, neural network and other algorithms [mathematical models] that use Doppler radar data. The data are integrated with other weather sensor data to guide forecasters.[65]

NSSL researchers chose Georgia for testing this system for an important reason. The state has experienced a number of killer tornadoes, such as the one that killed twenty people and injured ninety others inside a church during Palm Sunday services on March 27, 1994. Gene Greneker of Georgia Tech University's Severe Storm Research Center said that their aim was to optimize NG-WDSS for Georgia's environment:

> Tornadoes in Georgia and elsewhere in the Southeast are often short-lived events. They can come and go in 10 minutes, as opposed to an hour in Kansas. As a result, the radar signal processing may need to be set slightly

Can Your Pet Forecast Tornadoes?

Many people have observed that before a tornado arrives, their pets seem to recognize that something is about to happen. In fact, people who have survived tornadoes, particularly those who live on farms, sometimes tell stories about how oddly their dogs or horses acted before the tornado arrived.

How helpful this behavior is as a true indicator of approaching severe weather is a matter of debate. But Canadian tornado researchers and storm chasers Arjen and Jerrine Verkaik, in their book *Under the Whirlwind: Everything You Need to Know About Tornadoes but Didn't Know Who to Ask*, feel that there are benefits to watching animals closely when severe weather threatens.

Most animals are sensitive to their environment, including sudden or exceptional weather changes. Their awareness and reactions are not necessarily consistent or foolproof, but when they do sense a storm coming they may give us early warning. They may become restless or edgy, seek comfort and safety, or behave strangely. Horses and dogs may hear things well beyond our hearing range, even before there is any visible sign of danger, so your dog may truly be your best friend in the event of a tornado. But don't count on it. Some animals respond only to more immediate and apparent dangers. . . . It is possible that some tales of "doggie early warning" are exaggerated by hindsight. Behaviour we would normally have forgotten may assume undue significance after a tornado occurs. Even so, there is much to gain (and nothing to lose) to being attentive to an animal's behaviour. It may provide an early-warning system, and it will certainly bring us closer to our pets that bring us so much pleasure in our lives.

A pet's behavior may indicate an approaching tornado. Some people think animals have the ability to sense the impending danger of a storm.

different from those that were developed for the Great Plains states where the NG-WDSS was first developed and tested.[66]

Georgia Tech University scientists are also studying a recent theory about tornado formation that researchers feel holds a certain amount of promise. Lightning, the process of discharging electricity contained within clouds, may be a key to tornadogenesis and provide another means of forecasting in the future.

Lightning Striking Again and Again

The Georgia Tech University scientists are part of a group of researchers delving into the role of lightning in tornadogenesis. Their study measures electrical discharge from cloud-to-cloud lightning strikes, in the hope that they can confirm the theory that increasing amounts of electrical discharge indicates tornado formation. At the same time, other scientists from across the country are studying lightning to see if they can help advance tornado forecasting.

A partnership of the National Aeronautics and Space Administration (NASA), the NOAA, and the Massachusetts Institute of Technology's Lincoln Laboratories is using a combination of ground- and space-based weather-monitoring equipment. Their initial data documents nearly a dozen cases in which lightning rates greatly increased as tornadic storms developed. About thirty minutes before a storm produces a tornado, the lightning activity increases as the storm's updrafts get stronger. As the lightning from cloud to cloud increases, the cloud-to-ground lightning decreases. About ten minutes before a tornado is produced, lightning begins to diminish as updrafts weaken and the tornado starts to form.

However, this lightning is generally invisible to the naked eye of an observer on the ground. The scientists in charge of the monitoring studies are relying on NASA's Lightning Imaging Sensor (LIS) flying aboard a NASA satellite in low earth orbit. The LIS has counted up to sixty flashes per minute for storms that produced tornadoes, as compared with nontornadic thunderstorms that produce only a few flashes per minute. According to Steve Goodman, a researcher at the Global Hydrology and Climate Center managed by NASA's Marshall Space Flight Center in Huntsville, Alabama:

> Our studies show a very big spike in the lightning's flash rate prior to formation of a tornado. It's an early clue for weather forecasters to take a more detailed look at other storm characteristics with radar, and perhaps a chance for them to get warnings out earlier, saving more lives. . . . We don't have enough data yet to say how often the high flash rate precedes tornado development. But looking at this lightning signature can help pinpoint storms that are likely candidates, and that can make a big difference.[67]

Multiple cloud-to-ground and cloud-to-cloud lightning strikes during a nighttime thunderstorm.

So far, the technique of observing lightning flashes seems to work for both supercell and nonsupercell thunderstorms that produce tornadoes. But before this information can be put to practical use, equipment similar to LIS units would need to be installed in geostationary satellites and the means would have to be found to distribute this information to forecasters as quickly as possible.

However, other scientists are not relying on satellites to study lightning and its possible relationship to tornadogenesis. Government, private, and university researchers conducted a project called STEPS

(Severe Thunderstorm Electrification and Precipitation Studies) during the late spring and early summer of 2000. Using a combination of high-tech and low-tech instrumentation, the STEPS teams studied several storms on the western Great Plains with interesting results.

Project STEPS

The scientists involved with STEPS worked on the high plains of western Kansas and eastern Colorado in hopes of surrounding a thunderstorm and monitoring its development both on the ground and in the stratosphere. One of their goals was to get as close to thunderstorms as possible with their equipment, which included a specially modified airplane originally designed in the 1950s for pilot training.

Today the airplane is specially modified to withstand lightning strikes and damaging hail. Pilot Tom Warner was able to fly into thunderstorms to collect lightning data on film for STEPS. Walter Lyons, president of FMA Research in Fort Collins, Colorado, flew along to record unique lightning activity found in the stratosphere above the storms. These giant flashes of red light, sometimes called sprites, occur between fifty and sixty miles high, and Lyons captured them on film with special low-light cameras similar to night vision goggles.

The role that sprites play in tornadogenesis is not yet known. The STEPS project is studying the film of this electrical activity to create a larger picture of the atmosphere and thunderstorm behavior. The scientists also set up fifteen listening stations across the study area to plot energy pulses in the storm cells to create a three-dimensional map of lightning activity. The information about where and when electrical activity occurs within a thunderstorm may "eventually improve forecasting of severe weather,"[68] according to David Rust, a researcher with the NSSL.

The STEPS project also featured some definitely low-tech equipment, including vehicles with large nets on their roofs to catch hailstones for further study. These vehicles may have drawn unbelieving stares from observers, but scientists are often used to having to explain their methods to nonscientists. Recent instruments used to study tornadoes have included "turtles," "supersnails," and "Dillo-cams." Each follows in the spirit of the retired TOTO, and all are helping scientists step into the future of tornado science.

Turtle Follows TOTO

As computerized equipment becomes smaller and faster, and as recording devices such as video cameras and weather-sensing equipment become more sophisticated, scientists are discovering that they no longer have to resort to a device the size of TOTO to record tornado information. In the last ten years, several professional and amateur scientists have developed instrumentation packages that weigh substantially less than TOTO's four hundred pounds.

The first of this new generation of recorders was the turtle. These large, chrome, dome-shaped hubcaplike instrument packages were developed and designed by University of Oklahoma researchers Fred Brock, Jim LaDue, Mark Shafer, and Glenn Lesins, and recorded much of the same information that TOTO did. But the turtles had a tremendous advantage over TOTO. The data was recorded digitally instead of on paper strips, and the units were extremely portable. They could also be built in large numbers and could be deployed in several areas across a tornado's path.

A turtle was first placed near a tornado in May 1988 in Oklahoma, but when researchers recovered the unit and attempted to study the recorded information, they found that the data had been damaged, perhaps by someone curious about the turtle's purpose. Meteorologists continued to use the turtles for the next ten years or so, including during Project VORTEX in 1994 and 1995. But no tornado ever passed directly over them, and their use has been discontinued.

The Dillo-Cam

The Dillo-cam, similar in shape to the turtle, was developed by storm chasers Charles Edwards and Casey Crosbie.

The Dillo-cam is a camcorder encased in lead-weighted fiberglass which can be left in the path of a tornado to record data.

Edwards says that he wanted to get a film record from up close to, or perhaps from inside, a tornado, and so developed the Dillo-cam, whose name combines "armadillo" and "camera." The instrument's shell resembles an armadillo in shape, but it is also an appropriate name for the lead-weighted fiberglass shell that protects the camcorder tucked inside. Edwards says, "Friends made fun of me, saying that it would never work [because scientists had been trying] to put instruments in a tornado for years without any direct hits."[69]

But their perseverance was rewarded on May 25, 1997, when Edwards and Crosbie successfully deployed the Dillo-cam in front of a tornado, which passed directly over the unit.

When they found the Dillo-cam the next day, it was battered and dented from its encounter with the tornado, but the video camera had recorded some spectacular video footage.

Edwards's newest model weighs about a hundred pounds and contains two video cameras plus instruments to record temperature, dew point air pressure, and wind speed. He has had several "near misses"[70] with it, including a tornado that dissipated in front of the camera in 1999. He continues to use this invention during his storm chases.

Snails and Supersnails

Frank Tatom, another inventor, set out to test a different aspect of tornadoes. People who have experienced tornadoes sometimes claim that the ground shook as the storm moved toward them. Tatom decided to find out if this actually occurs,

Will Global Warming Mean More Tornadoes?

One of the current topics of debate among scientists as well as the general public is the concept of global warming. This concept theorizes that the influence of humans is changing the climate of the earth, primarily through the burning of fossil fuels such as oil, gas, and coal. Burning these natural resources releases carbon dioxide and other gases into the atmosphere, creating a "greenhouse effect" by trapping the earth's heat in the atmosphere instead of letting it escape into space.

One argument often used as a demonstration that global warming exists, and is becoming more severe with each passing year, is the increasing number of severe weather events around the world, such as tornadoes, hurricanes, droughts, and floods. Those who call attention to global warming claim that these catastrophes point toward an environment out of balance.

However, tornado researcher Thomas P. Grazulis, in *The Tornado: Nature's Ultimate Windstorm*, writes:

in hopes that someday a warning system could be developed based on detecting this ground motion.

To measure this, Tatom developed a portable instrument package called the snail. Inside the snail are instruments designed to measure three parts of a short-duration seismic signal. Thus if mini-earthquakes were actually occurring, the snail could measure them. Although snails and turtles look very much alike, the main difference is that the snail includes a geophone, which is a sensor that measures ground movement.

Several storm chasers deployed their snails, and its successor, the supersnail (which includes a tilt meter to measure longer-duration earth movements), in the 1990s to test their operations. The data the instruments collected encouraged Tatom's company, Engineering Analysis, Inc., and its subsidiary VorTek LLC, to continue their research and development.

In the future, someone may try to relate the numbers of tornadoes, or tornado deaths, to human-induced global warming. Any such links of tornado activity with climate change of any kind should be treated with the greatest skepticism. The ingredients that go into the creation of a tornado are so varied and complex that they could never be an accurate indicator of climate change. Higher temperatures may or may not mean more tornadoes. More heat could mean more convection and more thunderstorms, but the latter could also produce heavier rainfall that can smother updrafts in torrential downpours. Higher temperatures may somehow drive the jet stream farther north away from the Great Plains and the Midwest. This might make drought more likely than tornado outbreaks.

Clearly, the relationship between severe weather and climate change requires further study. It is also clear that the debate over global warming will continue for years to come. Whether or not it exists, and whether or not it will bring more tornadoes, remains to be seen.

Today VorTek is committed to refining the supersnail concept and to continuing the theory of ground motion related to tornadoes. The company plans to fund distribution of company-owned supersnails to experienced storm chasers. The storm chasers will attempt to place the instruments in the path of tornadoes, and then return the units to VorTek at the end of the season so the seismic data can be analyzed. VorTek is also pursuing partnerships with the NOAA, FEMA, and Georgia Tech's Severe Storms Research Center to advance supersnail research. The company ultimately hopes that they can work with residences and entire communities in "tornado-prone areas"[71] to deploy a network of permanently installed supersnails as tornado forecasting systems.

What Does the Future Hold?

VorTek's tornado forecasting systems, so far, are only a dream and represent a nonmeteorological method of dealing with severe weather. While the firm's ideas may seem farfetched, it is important to remember that even traditional meteorological methods of investigation have not mastered tornado forecasting.

Perhaps the key to tornado forecasting lies within a combination of technologies and techniques. Satellite-based lightning detectors, ground-based observations, radar-based data, Internet-based communications, and as-yet-undeveloped devices may yet combine to forecast tornadoes with the same degree of confidence associated with precipitation today. Howard Bluestein looks forward to a day when forecasters can use finely crafted computer models to "predict that, for example, 'in four hours, in Cleveland County, in central Oklahoma, there will be a sixty percent chance of hail larger than three-quarters of an inch in diameter, and surface winds greater than fifty-five mph.'"[72] But that day has not yet arrived.

In the meantime scientists and amateurs alike continue to be fascinated by tornadoes and continue to work toward a greater understanding of them. Thomas Grazulis says, "I and thousands of others wait in anticipation for each tornado season. Each season will be unique. The combination of timing, location, size, and intensity of outbreaks will be different from those of any other year."[73] Bluestein adds, "Our quest for discovery has not taken away from the respect we have for the awesome power the tornado harbors, nor the thrill of viewing the violent motions in the tornado or the beauty of the storm. We eagerly await the next act in the atmospheric play starring the tornado."[74] And the National Severe Storms Laboratory's

Scientists still have not mastered tornado forecasting but they are getting closer with new technologies and new techniques.

Erik Rasmussen, describing his desire to unlock the secrets of tornadoes, says, "It's something I really need to do. It satisfies my soul."[75]

The dedication of these professionals, as well as the advances made in understanding tornadoes in the last fifty years, bodes well for the future. A truly reliable system of tornado forecasting may be in the near future. That will be good news, as the next outbreak may only be a day away.

Epilogue: Hoisington, Kansas, April 21, 2001

There have been tremendous advances in weather forecasting and weather awareness since the Super Outbreak of thunderstorms and tornadoes of April 1974. A network of weather observers and storm spotters blankets the United States. Sophisticated technologies, such as Doppler radar systems and geostationary satellites, help meteorologists try to make sense of weather features and developing patterns. Experienced scientists have delved deep into the mysteries surrounding the formation and behavior of tornadoes, and they can forecast their approach with better accuracy than ever before. Their expertise continues to help prepare citizens for potentially dangerous weather, and their timely warnings may have saved countless numbers of lives.

Yet even with the most sophisticated technology and timely warning, lives are still lost due to tornadoes. The tornado that struck Hoisington, Kansas, on April 21, 2001, was one such storm.

On that particular Saturday night, Hoisington residents were aware that severe weather was in the area, but many thought that the worst of the thunderstorms would pass north of town. One resident told his wife that if there was any danger, the town's warning sirens would go off, giving them plenty of time to seek shelter. When winds started to shake the house, she went alone to the basement of the house. She survived the storm; her husband did not.

The couple's home was destroyed. Almost three hundred other structures were demolished or damaged as the tornado cut a swath six blocks wide and a mile long through Hoisington. According to the Associated Press account of the storm:

The roof was blown off the high school, the local hospital had to be evacuated and the Dairy Queen was destroyed while several people took shelter in a walk-in freezer. High school students interrupted their prom to go to a shelter. Hoisington area officials had been watching the approaching storm for more than an hour. The local sheriff said that he and another officer had been observing the storm from the city limits but had seen only low clouds and lightning. He said later, "Nobody saw this tornado. Nobody saw it coming."[76]

A woman stands next to the car that landed in the basement of her home after a tornado ripped through Hoisington, Kansas, in April 2001.

Clearly, even with all the advancements in severe weather and tornado forecasting that have occurred in the last twenty-five years, there are still tornadoes that develop without anyone seeing them. The Hoisington tornado serves as a reminder of the need to remain alert to potential danger even in the absence of official forecasts of tornado development.

Perhaps someday science will find a way to modify the weather or reduce the impact of severe weather. Future technologies may provide greater lead time for forecasting local details of dangerous weather, so that alert citizens can take shelter before the storms strike, further reducing the potential loss of life.

However, such ideas today remain in the domain of science fiction and not science fact. Despite all the tools, training, and technology that exist today, citizens must remain ever alert to the potential for severe thunderstorms, because they never know when the next tornado will strike.

Notes

Introduction: Xenia, Ohio, April 3, 1974

1. Quoted in Jack Williams, *The Weather Book*. New York: Random House, 1997, p. 138.

Chapter 1: The Coming Fury

2. Roger Edwards, "The Online Tornado FAQ: Frequently Asked Questions About Tornadoes," NOAA Storm Prediction Center, May 6, 1999, p. 2. www.spc.noaa.gov/faq/tornado.

3. Thomas P. Grazulis, *The Tornado: Nature's Ultimate Windstorm*. Norman: University of Oklahoma Press, 2001, p. 75.

4. Erik Rasmussen and Paul Markowski, "Tornado Forecasting," www.NSSL.NOAA.gov/~erik/www/SSR/Tornadoes/Forecasting/TforEZ_set.htm.

5. *Fergus (Ontario) News-Record*, July 26, 1906; quoted in Grazulis, pp. 21–22.

6. Grazulis, *Tornado*, p. 16.

7. Weather Channel Special Reports, "Inside Tornadoes," p. 1. www.weather.com/newscenter/specialreports/tornado/inside/about.html.

8. Edwards, "Online Tornado FAQ," p. 3.

9. Grazulis, *Tornado*, p. 254.

10. Grazulis, *Tornado*, p. 261.

11. Quoted in Ben Fenwick, "Storm Chasers Tracked Deadly U.S. Twister," Reuters, May 6, 1999, pp. 1–2. www.trv-psitech.com/tornado.htm.

Chapter 2: Tornadogenesis: The Tornado Forms

12. NOAA, "Storm Spotter Field Guide," March 6, 2001, p. 9, www.srh.noaa.gov/oun/skywarn/spotterguide.html.

13. Michael Branick, "Technical Memorandum NWS SR-145: A Comprehensive Glossary of Weather Terms for Storm Spotters," September 1996. www.srh.noaa.gov/oun/severewx/branick2.html.

14. Branick, "A Comprehensive Glossary of Weather Terms."

15. Charles A. Doswell III, Alan R. Moller, and Harold E. Brooks, "Storm Spotting and Public Awareness Since the First Tornado Forecasts of 1948," *Weather and Forecasting*, vol. 14, no. 4, August 1999, p. 546.

16. Doswell, Moller, and Brooks, "Storm Spotting," p. 544.

17. U.S. Department of Commerce, NWS Memphis, "Severe Weather Summary of March 1st Tornadoes," March 11, 1997. www.srh.noaa.gov/ftproot/meg/html/summary2.html.

18. Quoted in Amanda Alexander, "Stormy Weather Returns to Area," *Aberdeen American-News*, July 20, 2001, p. 1A.

19. Howard B. Bluestein, *Tornado Alley: Monster Storms of the Great Plains*. New York: Oxford University Press 1999, p. 67.

20. Bluestein, *Tornado Alley*, p. 154.

21. Quoted in Grazulis, *Tornado*, p. 100.

22. Quoted in Grazulis, *Tornado*, p. 101.

23. Quoted in Grazulis, *Tornado*, p. 101.

Chapter 3: The Tornado Strikes

24. Quoted in Judi Boland, "Storms Attract Spotters, Trackers, Chasers and the Curious," *Topeka Capital-Journal*, June 17, 2001, p. 1. http://cjonline.com/stories/061701/new_tornadochasers.shtml.

25. Bluestein, *Tornado Alley*, p. 124.

26. Herb Stein, "Storm Chasers Face the Powerful Forces of Nature," *National Geographic News*, June 11, 2001, p. 1. http://news.nationalgeographic.com/news/2001/06/061 1_ stormchaser3.html.

27. KWTV, "Val Castor: Senior Storm Tracker," p. 1. www.kwtv.com/news/talent/castor.htm.

28. Edwards, "Online Tornado FAQ," p. 5.

29. Quoted in Kansas State Historical Society, "Tornado Photographs," 1997, p. 1. www.kshs.org/cool2/cooltorn.htm.

30. Edwards, "Online Tornado FAQ," p. 3.

31. Quoted in Grazulis, *Tornado*, p. 202.

32. Doswell, Moller, and Brooks, "Storm Spotting." p. 9.

33. Doswell, Moller, and Brooks, "Storm Spotting," p. 10.

34. NOAA Storm Prediction Center, "Watch #464," May 30, 1998. www.spc.noaa.gov/archive/products/watch98/ww0499.zip.

35. NOAA Storm Prediction Center, "Mesoscale Discussion #0518," May 30, 1998. www.spc.noaa.gov/archive/produx98/053098.zip.

36. NOAA Storm Prediction Center, "Watch #469," May 30, 1998. www.spc.noaa.gov/archive/products/watch98/ww0499.zip.

37. Quoted in David Kranz and Rob Swenson, "Spencer Grieves 6 Deaths, Loss of Belongings," *Sioux Falls Argus Leader,* May 31, 1998, p. 1. www.argusleader.com/tornado/index.html#article.

38. Quoted in David Kranz, "Governor Optimistic, but Residents Doubtful," *Sioux Falls Argus Leader*, June 1,

1998, p. 1. www.argusleader.com/tornado/index.html# article2.

Chapter 4: Aftermath

39. Quoted in South Dakota Public Broadcasting, "May 30, 1998: Spencer SD. The Rebuilding Process," 1999. www.sdpb.org/spencer/rebuilding_process.htm.

40. Quoted in Jerrine Verkaik and Arjen Verkaik, *Under the Whirlwind: Everything You Need to Know About Tornadoes but Didn't Know Who to Ask.* Elmwood, Ontario: Whirlwind Books, 1997, pp. 18–19.

41. Quoted in Federal Emergency Management Agency, "NSSL Scientist Works with FEMA in the Aftermath," *NSSL Briefings.*www.nssl.noaa.gov/briefings/vol2_no4/ fema.html.

42. Martin Lisius, "The Spencer SD Tornado of 30 May 1998: Martin Lisius' Storm Intercept Account," 1998. www.spc.noaa.gov/misc/spencer/mlchase.htm.

43. Rich Curry, "Tinker Responds to Tornado Aftermath," *Airforce News*, May 4, 1999. www.af.mil.gov/news/ May1999/n19990504 _990863.html.

44. Curry, "Tinker Responds to Tornado Aftermath."

45. Quoted in Verkaik and Verkaik, *Under the Whirlwind*, p. 24.

46. Quoted in Verkaik and Verkaik, *Under the Whirlwind,* p. 35.

47. *Sioux Falls Argus Leader*, "How You Can Help," p. 1. www.argusleader.com/tornado/donations.html.

48. Lydia Carrico, "Some Donations Remain Unspent," *Owensboro (Kentucky) Messenger-Inquirer*, January 3, 2001. www.messenger-inquirer.com/tornado/2582478.htm.

49. Quoted in Carrico, "Some Donations Remain Unspent."

50. Reuters, "Millions in Tornado Losses," May 5, 1999. http://archive.abcnews.go.com/sections/business/Daily News/tornado_insurance990505.html.

51. Quoted in James Mayse, "Residents Are Offered More Help," *Owensboro (Kentucky) Messenger-Inquirer*, January 12, 2001. www.messenger-inquirer.com/tornado/1648304.htm.

52. Quoted in James Mayse, "Storm Survivors: Victims Recalled Tornado's Fury," *Owensboro (Kentucky) Messenger-Inquirer*, January 3, 2001. www.messenger-inquirer.com/tornado/2582837.htm.

Chapter 5: What Can Be Done?:
A Glimpse into the Future

53. Grazulis, *Tornado*, p. 288.

54. Grazulis, *Tornado*, p. 288.

55. Edwards, "Online Tornado FAQ," p. 5.

56. Weather Channel Special Reports, "Awesome Power: Furious Company," p. 3. www.weather.com/newscenter/specialreports/tornado/awesome/company.html.

57. Grazulis, *Tornado*, p. 288.

58. Edwards, "Online Tornado FAQ," p. 5.

59. Bluestein, *Tornado Alley*, pp. 159–60.

60. Verkaik and Verkaik, *Under the Whirlwind*, p. 151.

61. Quoted in Grazulis, *Tornado*, p. 249.

62. Verkaik and Verkaik, *Under the Whirlwind*, p. 151.

63. Gary A. England, *Weathering the Storm: Tornadoes, Television, and Turmoil*. Norman: University of Oklahoma Press, 1996, p. 151.

64. Grazulis, *Tornado*, p. 249.

65. *Fayetteville (Georgia) Citizen*, "New Tornado Forecasting System Being Tested in Peachtree City," June 2, 1999. www.thecitizennews.com/main/archive-990602/news/in-09.html.

66. Quoted in *Fayetteville (Georgia) Citizen*, "New Tornado Forecasting System Being Tested in Peachtree City."

67. Quoted in Kim Lanier, "More Data Needed for Forecasting," *Mobile (Alabama) Register*, April 30, 2000. www.al.com/news/mobile/Apr2000/30-a334612a.html.

68. Quoted in Roxana Hegeman, "Modern-Day High Technology Revamps Weather Forecasting," *Norman (Oklahoma) Transcript*, June 4, 2000. www.nssl.noaa.gov/headlines/steps.html.

69. Charles Edwards, "The Bear's Cage," *Cloud 9 Tours*. www.cloud9tours.com/bear/.

70. Edwards, "The Bear's Cage."

71. VorTek LLC, "Executive Summary," September 24, 2001. http://vortek.home.mindspring.com.

72. Bluestein, *Tornado Alley*, p. 155.

73. Grazulis, *Tornado*, p. 289.

74. Bluestein, *Tornado Alley,* p. 162.

75. Quoted in Williams, *The Weather Book*, p. 133.

Epilogue: Hoisington, Kansas, April 21, 2001

76. Associated Press, "Kansas Man Dies in Freak Tornado," *The Great Falls Tribune*, April 23, 2001, p. 2A.

Glossary

column: In meteorology, a rotating air mass that may be vertical, horizontal, or tilted.

downburst: A violent rush of straight-line winds that streak from a thunderstorm and spread out in all directions when it hits the ground.

jet stream: Relatively narrow bands of high-speed winds (up to 150 mph) in the upper atmosphere. Over North America the jet stream flows generally from west to east but also can drift great distances north and south.

mesocyclone: A rotating column of low-pressure air that occurs in thunderstorms and that may contribute to the development of a tornado.

National Oceanic and Atmospheric Administration (NOAA): An agency of the U.S. Department of Commerce that describes and predicts changes in the earth's environment and conserves and manages the United States' coastal and marine resources.

National Severe Storms Laboratory (NSSL): A branch of the NOAA's Office of Oceanic and Atmospheric Research that investigates all aspects of severe and hazardous weather and works in partnership with the National Weather Service to improve the lead time and accuracy of severe weather warnings and forecasts. Formerly the National Severe Storms Forecast Center (NSSFC).

National Weather Service (NWS): A bureau of the U.S. Department of Commerce that is responsible for the tracking, forecasting, and compiling of statistics related to weather across the nation.

rain-free base: When seen from the ground, a dark, horizontal cloud base with no visible precipitation beneath it, although it may contain rain or hail not visible to a ground observer.

SKYWARN: A U.S.-based nationwide network of trained severe weather observers who work in partnership with the National Weather Service (NWS).

Storm Prediction Center (SPC): A branch of the NWS that provides timely and accurate forecasts and watches for severe thunderstorms and tornadoes across the United States.

supercell: A thunderstorm with a persistent rotating updraft that often produces severe thunderstorms and tornadoes.

tornado: A rapidly rotating column of air in contact with the ground. Wind speeds can reach over three hundred miles an hour.

tornado warning: An alert issued by the NWS when severe weather is in progress or has been reported by observers.

tornado watch: An alert issued by the NWS when conditions are favorable for severe weather in a particular area.

tornadogenesis: The evolution of a tornado, from thunderstorm to tornado touchdown.

updraft: A rising column of air in the atmosphere.

vortex: The center of a column of air.

For Further Reading

Fred Andrews, Lisa Schwimmer, and Kathy Zaun, *Natural Disasters: Volcanoes, Earthquakes, Hurricanes, Droughts, Tornadoes and Floods.* Torrance, CA: Good Apple, 1997. Includes activities designed to introduce students to forces of nature.

Jules Archer, *Tornado!* Nature's Disasters series. New York: Crestwood House, 1991. This slim volume provides a good introduction to tornadoes, although some information is now outdated, particularly concerning Doppler radar systems.

Jean Craighead George, *One Day in the Prairie.* New York: Thomas Y. Crowell, 1986. A richly illustrated volume that deals more with the overall ecosystem of the Great Plains than with tornadoes specifically but does describe an encounter with a tornado.

Michael H. Mogil, *Tornadoes.* Stillwater, MN: Voyageur Press, 2001. Meteorologist Mogil presents a combination of tornado narratives and reader-friendly descriptions of cutting-edge technology.

Kevin Moore and Jack Challoner, *Eyewitness: Hurricane & Tornado.* New York: Dorling Kindersley, 2000. Covers a wider range of weather phenomena than the title suggests but has the Eyewitness series hallmark illustrations and interesting facts.

Neil Morris, *Hurricanes & Tornadoes*. New York: Crabtree Publishing, 1999. Morris presents the fury and power of extreme weather, along with modern scientific methods of predicting and preparing for severe weather.

Victoria Sherrow, *Plains Outbreak Tornadoes: Killer Twisters*. Springfield, NJ: Enslow Publishers, 1998. This book concentrates on the tornado outbreak of April 1991, with information on tornado formation and accounts from survivors.

Seymour Simon, *Tornadoes*. New York: HarperCollins Children's Books, 2001. Concise text and large photographs illustrate the development and aftermath of tornadoes, as well as meteorologists at work.

Jack Williams, *The Weather Book*. New York: Random House, 1997. Williams covers a variety of weather phenomena, from the everyday to the uncommon, and includes interviews with weather professionals and scientists.

Brenda Wyma, *Weather*. Cypress, CA: Creative Teaching Press, 1995. Activities build upon the scientific method and the scientific process to investigate weather variables.

Works Consulted

Books

Howard B. Bluestein, *Tornado Alley: Monster Storms of the Great Plains*. New York: Oxford University Press, 1999. University of Oklahoma researcher, storm chaser, and photographer Bluestein highlights a number of scientific advancements in tornado research.

Gary A. England, *Weathering the Storm: Tornadoes, Television, and Turmoil*. Norman: University of Oklahoma Press, 1996. Meteorologist England works for KWTV in Oklahoma City and concentrates his narrative on his experiences with tornadoes in Oklahoma but includes interesting tidbits about tornado research and television politics.

Thomas P. Grazulis, *The Tornado: Nature's Ultimate Windstorm*. Norman: University of Oklahoma Press, 2001. Grazulis, director of the Tornado Project, presents fascinating insights into the development of tornado research as well as descriptions of a number of landmark tornado events.

Eric Pinder, *Tying Down the Wind: Adventures in the Worst Weather on Earth*. New York: Tarcher/Putnam, 2000. Pinder's interest in severe weather began with a stint as a meteorologist at the observatory atop New Hampshire's Mount Washington, and this book illustrates a number of his experiences with nature's extremes.

Bob Reiss, *The Coming Storm: Extreme Weather and Our Terrifying Future*. New York: Hyperion, 2001. Reiss uses documentary evidence and interviews with elected officials, scientists, and members of the general public to support the premise that global warming exists and is influencing the planet's weather.

Jerrine Verkaik and Arjen Verkaik, *Under the Whirlwind: Everything You Need to Know About Tornadoes but Didn't Know Who to Ask*. Elmwood, Ontario: Whirlwind Books, 1997. Husband-and-wife team Arjen and Jerrine Verkaik are storm chasers and photographers who share their stories about tornadoes they have encountered across North America.

Periodicals

Amanda Alexander, "Stormy Weather Returns to Area," *Aberdeen American-News*, July 20, 2001.

Associated Press, "10 People Known Dead in Tornadoes," *Great Falls Tribune*, October 7, 2001.

———, "Kansas Man Dies in Freak Tornado," *The Great Falls Tribune*, April 23, 2001.

Howard B. Bluestein, "A History of Severe-Storm Intercept Field Programs," *Weather and Forecasting*, vol. 14, no. 4, August 1999.

———, "A Tornadic Supercell over Elevated, Complex Terrain: The Divide, Colorado Storm of 12 July 1996," *Monthly Weather Review*, vol. 128, no. 3, March 2000.

Howard B. Bluestein et al., "Doppler Radar Analysis of the Northfield, Texas, Tornado of 25 May 1994," *Monthly Weather Review*, vol. 125, no. 2, February 1997.

Marlene Bradford, "Historical Roots of Modern Tornado Forecasts and Warnings," *Weather and Forecasting*, vol. 14, no. 4, August 1999.

Pete Browning, John T. Weaver, and Bernadette Connell, "The Moberly, Missouri, Tornado of 4 July 1995," *Weather and Forecasting*, vol. 12, no. 4, December 1997.

Chris Cappella, "Storm Troopers," *Weatherwise*, November/December 2000.

Charles A. Doswell III, Alan R. Moller, and Harold E. Brooks, "Storm Spotting and Public Awareness Since the First Tornado Forecasts of 1948," *Weather and Forecasting*, vol. 14, no. 4, August 1999.

David C. Dowell and Howard B. Bluestein, "Analysis of a Supercell During Tornadogenesis," *Monthly Weather Review*, vol. 125, no. 10, October 1997.

G.S. Forbes and H.B. Bluestein, "Tornadoes, Tornadic Thunderstorms, and Photogrammetry: A Review of the Contributions of T. Theodore Fujita," *Bulletin of the American Meteorological Society*, vol. 82, no. 1, January 2001.

Robert Henson, "Billion-Dollar Twister," *Scientific American: Weather*, vol. 11, no. 1, spring 2000.

Michael A. Magsig and John T. Snow, "Long-Distance Debris Transport by Tornadic Thunderstorms. Part I: The 7 May 1995 Supercell Thunderstorm," *Monthly Weather Review*, vol. 126, no. 6, June 1998.

Daniel McCarthy and Joseph T. Schaefer, "Tornadoes of 2000," *Weatherwise*, March/April 2001.

———, "Twisters Go Urban," *Weatherwise*, March/April 2000.

J.R. McDonald, "T. Theodore Fujita: His Contribution to Tornado Knowledge Through Damage Documentation and the Fujita Scale," *Bulletin of the American Meteorological Society*, vol. 82, no. 1, January 2001.

Erik N. Rasmussen et al., "The Association of Significant Tornadoes with a Baroclinic Boundary on 2 June 1995," *Monthly Weather Review*, vol. 128, no. 1, January 2000.

Will Schmid et al., "The Origin of Severe Winds in a Tornadic Bow-Echo Storm over Northern Switzerland," *Monthly Weather Review,* vol. 128, no. 1, January 2000.

Roger M. Wakimoto and Chinghwang Liu, "The Garden City, Kansas, Storm During VORTEX 95. Part II: The Wall Cloud and Tornado," *Monthly Weather Review*, vol. 126, no. 2, February 1998.

Roger M. Wakimoto, Chinghwang Liu, and Huaqing Cai, "The Garden City, Kansas, Storm During VORTEX 95. Part I: Overview of the Storm's Life Cycle and Mesocyclogenesis," *Monthly Weather Review,* vol. 126, no. 2, February 1998.

J.W. Wilson and R.M. Wakimoto, "The Discovery of the Downburst: T.T. Fujita's Contribution," *Bulletin of the American Meteorological Society*, vol. 82, no. 1, January 2001.

Internet Sources

Judi Boland, "Storms Attract Spotters, Trackers, Chasers, and the Curious," *Topeka Capital-Journal*, June 17, 2001. http://cjonline.com/stories/061701/new_tornadochasers.shtml.

Michael Branick, "Technical Memorandum NWS SR-145: A Comprehensive Glossary of Weather Terms for Storm Spotters," September 1996. www.srh.noaa.gov/oun/severewx/branick2.html.

Harold E. Brooks and Charles A. Doswell III, "Normalized Damage from Tornadoes in the United States: 1890–1999," September 2000. www.nssl.noaa.gov/~brooks/damage/tdam1.html.

Lydia Carrico, "Some Donations Remain Unspent," *Owensboro (Kentucky) Messenger-Inquirer*, January 3, 2001. www.messenger-inquirer.com/tornado/2582478.htm.

Rich Curry, "Tinker [Air Force Base] Responds to Tornado Aftermath," *Air Force News*, May 4, 1999. www.af.mil.gov/news/May1999/n19990504_990863.html.

Robert Davies-Jones, "Tornadoes: The Storms that Spawn Twisters Are Now Largely Understood, but Mysteries Still Remain About How These Violent Vortices Form," *Scientific American*, August 1995. www.sciam.com/explorations/0895davies.html.

Charles Edwards, "The Bear's Cage," *Cloud 9 Tours.* www.cloud9tours.com/bear/.

Roger Edwards, "Observations and Damage Analysis of the Spencer SD Tornado of 30 May 1998," May 31, 1999. www.spc.noaa.gov/misc/spencer/index.html.

————, "The Online Tornado FAQ: Frequently Asked Questions About Tornadoes," NOAA Storm Prediction Center, May 6, 1999. www.spc.noaa.gov/faq/tornado.

Fayetteville (Georgia) Citizen, "New Tornado Forecasting System Being Tested in Peachtree City," June 2, 1999. www.thecitizennews.com/main/archive-990602/news/in-09.html.

Federal Emergency Management Agency, "NSSL Scientist Works with FEMA in the Aftermath," *NSSL Briefings,* n.d. www.nssl.noaa.gov/briefings/vol2_no4/fema.html.

————, "Spencer South Dakota Devastated, Day County Flooded," June 2, 1998. www.fema.gov/diz98/d1218n01.htm.

Ben Fenwick, "Storm Chasers Tracked Deadly U.S. Twister," Reuters, May 6, 1999. www.trv-psitech.com/tornado.htm.

Roxana Hegeman, "Modern-Day High Technology Revamps Weather Forecasting," *Norman (Oklahoma) Transcript*, June 4, 2000. www.nssl.noaa.gov/headlines/steps.html.

IMT Insurance, "History," 1999. www.imtins.com/history/history.htm.

Kansas State Historical Society, "Tornado Photographs," 1997. www.kshs.org/cool2/cooltorn.htm.

David Kranz, "Governor Optimistic, but Residents Doubtful," *Sioux Falls Argus Leader*, June 1, 1998. www.argusleader.com/tornado/index.html#article2.

David Kranz and Rob Swenson, "Spencer Grieves 6 Deaths, Loss of Belongings," *Sioux Falls Argus Leader*, May 31, 1998. www.argusleader.com/tornado/index.html#article.

KWTV, "Val Castor: Senior Storm Tracker," n.d. www.kwtv.com/news/talent/castor.htm.

Kim Lanier, "More Data Needed for Forecasting," *Mobile (Alabama) Register,* April 30, 2000. www.al.com/news/mobile/Apr2000/30-a334612a.html.

Martin Lisius, "The Spencer SD Tornado of 30 May 1998: Martin Lisius' Storm Intercept Account," 1998. www.spc.noaa.gov/misc/spencer/mlchase.htm.

James Mayse, "Residents Are Offered More Help," *Owensboro (Kentucky) Messenger-Inquirer,* January 12, 2001. www.messenger-inquirer.com/tornado/1648304.htm.

———, "Storm Survivors: Victims Recalled Tornado's Fury," *Owensboro (Kentucky) Messenger-Inquirer*, January 3, 2001. www.messenger-inquirer.com/tornado/2582837.htm.

National Science Foundation, "Mobile Doppler Radar Instruments Edge Closer to Swirling Funnel Clouds: This Week's Oklahoma Tornadoes Provide Highest-Resolution-Ever Data," May 10, 1999. www.sciencedaily.com/print/05/990510064538.htm.

National Severe Storms Laboratory, "Studying Devastating Storms in the Heart of 'Tornado Alley,'" January 2001. www.nssl.noaa.gov/who/onepager.html.

National Weather Service, "Tornadoes . . . Nature's Most Violent Storms," September 1992. http://205.156.54.206/om/brochures/tornado.htm.

NOAA, "Storm Spotter Guide," March 6, 2001. www.srh.noaa.gov/oun/skywarn/spotterguide.html.

———, "Project Helps Scientists Understand Tornadoes," February 8, 2000. www.usatoday.com/weather/wvor2.htm.

NOAA Storm Prediction Center, "Mesoscale Discussion #0518," May 30, 1998. www.spc.noaa.gov/archive/produx98/053098.zip.

————, "Watch #464," May 30, 1998. www.spc.noaa.gov/archive/products/watch98/ww0499.zip.

————, "Watch #469," May 30, 1998. www.spc.noaa.gov/archive/products/watch98/ww0499.zip.

North Central Texas Council of Governments, "Tornado Damage Risk Assessment—Dallas Fort Worth Metroplex," Summer 2000. www.dfwinfo.com/weather/study/summary/summary.asp.

Owensboro (Kentucky) Messenger-Inquirer, "Tornado 2000: Tornado Anniversary," January 2000. www.messenger-inquirer.com/index/tornado.htm.

Erik Rasmussen and Paul Markowski, "Tornado Forecasting." http://mrd3.nssl.ncar.edu/-eras/www/SSR/Tornadoes/Forecasting/TforEZ_set.html.

Reuters, "Millions in Tornado Losses," May 5, 1999. http://archive.abcnews.go.com/sections/business/DailyNews/tornado_insurance990505.html.

Sioux Falls Argus Leader, "How You Can Help," www.argusleader.com/tornado/donations.html.

South Dakota Public Broadcasting, "May 30, 1998: Spencer, SD. The Rebuilding Process," 1999. www.sdpb.org/spencer/rebuilding_process.htm.

Herb Stein, "Storm Chasers Face the Powerful Forces of Nature," *National Geographic News*, June 11, 2001. http://news.nationalgeographic.com/news/2001/06/0611_stormchaser3.html.

Tornado Project, "The Fujita Scale of Tornado Intensity," 1999. www.tornadoproject.com.

University of Arkansas, "A Hard Wind Is Gonna Blow: Minimizing the Destruction from Tornadoes," March 20, 2000. www.sciencedaily.com/releases/2000/03/00032009 11506.htm.

University of Illinois, WW2010 Project, "Schematic Diagrams," 1997. ww2010.atmos.uiuc.edu/(Gh)/guides/mtr/svr/type/spr/sch.rxml.

U.S. Department of Commerce, NWS Memphis, "Severe Weather Summary of March 1st Tornadoes," March 11, 1997. www.srh.noaa.gov/ftproot/meg/html/summary2.html.

VorTek LLC, "Executive Summary," September 24, 2001. http://vortek.home.mindspring.com.

Weather Channel Special Reports, "Awesome Power: Fascinating History," n.d. www.weather.com/newscenter/specialreports/tornado/awesome/history.html.

———, "Awesome Power: Furious Company," n.d. www.weather.com/newscenter/specialreports/tornado/awesome/company.html.

———, "Inside Tornadoes," n.d. www.weather.com/news center/specialreports/tornado/inside/about.html.

———, "Inside Tornadoes: About Tornadoes," n.d. www.weather.com/newscenter/specialreports/tornado/inside/about.html.

———, "Inside Tornadoes: Fujita Scale," n.d. www.weather.com/newscenter/specialreports/tornado/inside/fujita.html.

Websites

There are hundreds of websites that are concerned with severe weather in general and tornadoes in particular. A few noteworthy selections are the following:

Dr. Charles Doswell III (www.nssl.noaa.gov/~doswell). Has a wide range of information about thunderstorms, tornadoes, storm chasing, and career choices from a National Severe Storm Laboratory researcher.

Dr. Erik Rasmussen (http://mrd3.nssl.ucar.edu/~eras/www/SSR/index.htm). Has a wealth of information about tornadogenesis, written for both the beginner and the advanced learner, as well as frequently asked questions and sources for further information.

SKYWARN (www.skywarn.org). The place to start for those interested in becoming storm spotters.

Storm Prediction Center (www.spc.noaa.gov). The NOAA's website has records of severe weather from across the United States, including archived data of weather watches and warnings from recent years.

The Tornado Project (www.tornadoproject.com). Includes a wide range of stories, activities, and scientific information about tornadoes. It also has links to a number of similar sites.

University of Illinois's *World Weather 2010* Project (http://ww2010.atmos.uiuc.edu/(Gh)/guides/mtr/svr/torn/home.rxml). Provides an amazing wealth of online information that integrates current and archived weather data with instructional resources. The tornadoes page has clear and concise information and stunning graphics.

Warner Brothers and Universal Pictures's *Twister* (movies.warnerbros.com/twister/cmp/swirl.html). Has a number of interesting aspects about tornadoes, the making of the film and its special effects, and interviews with cast and crew.

Weather Channel (www.weather.com). Offers up-to-the-minute coverage of weather across the globe, plus features about severe weather phenomena.

Index

Picture Credits

About the Author

Andrew A. Kling has been fascinated with weather for as long as he can remember. Kling lived in many areas throughout the United States during his career with the National Park Service, experiencing hailstorms, blizzards, and thunder-snow storms. During a seven-year period on the coast of North Carolina, Kling survived five hurricanes and numerous tropical storms.

As a park ranger, Kling facilitated public programs about hurricanes, blizzards, and other forms of severe weather; he also wrote and edited a park newspaper. From 1996 to 1999, he planned and implemented the visitor and public information services associated with the relocation of the Cape Hatteras Lighthouse in North Carolina. For the National Park Service, he cowrote *Sea, Sands, and Sounds: A Guide to Barrier Island Ecology and Geology,* a curriculum guide for middle school educators.

He currently lives in Montana, working as a freelance writer, editor, interpretive media developer, and consultant.